CHILDREN OF POVERTY

STUDIES ON THE EFFECTS OF SINGLE PARENTHOOD, THE FEMINIZATION OF POVERTY, AND HOMELESSNESS

edited by

STUART BRUCHEY
UNIVERSITY OF MAINE

A GARLAND SERIES

WOMEN'S CHOICES AND THE RISK OF POVERTY

CASE STUDIES OF BREAKING THE CYCLE

SHARON WARNER METHVIN

GARLAND PUBLISHING, INC.
NEW YORK & LONDON / 1997

Library of Congress Cataloging-in-Publication Data

Methvin, Sharon Warner, 1953–
    Women's choices and the risk of poverty : case studies of
breaking the cycle / Sharon Warner Methvin.
        p.   cm. — (Children of poverty)
    Includes bibliographical references and index.
    ISBN 0-8153-3049-9 (alk. paper)
    1. Poor women—Oklahoma—Case studies. 2. Minority
women—Oklahoma—Economic conditions—Case studies.
3. Women heads of households—Oklahoma—Economic conditions—Case studies. 4. Poverty—Oklahoma—Research—Case
studies. I. Title. II. Series.
HV1446.O5M47 1997
362.83'086'94209766—dc21   97-33179

Printed on acid-free, 250-year-life paper
Manufactured in the United States of America

May the lives of those humans and animals who suffer be touched by the energy of the story told herein and by the hearts of those who read it. Their suffering can be eased if each of us begins to act with intention and to see with feeling eyes.

Contents

Figures

Tables

Preface

Winter, 1985. . .I drive up in my late model Honda Wagon to what used to be a driveway and is now part of a weedy, litter strewn alley way entrance to a cluster of deteriorating row houses. The cats know my car; some of them come to greet me as I spread food on one of the porches, while others crouch warily in the shadows of crumbling doorways. The neighbors in surrounding houses go inside so I won't know that they exist. A person has recently joined the homeless cat colony because I see his clothes hanging on a porch rail. One day he and I almost run into each other as I turn the corner and catch him opening a tattered bag of food for the cats for which he too has begun to care. I sneak quietly away as a woman's children play in the dirt to amuse themselves. She keeps an eye on them through an open, unscreened kitchen door.

A few months later...I am called to check on an emaciated animal chained to a dog house at a rental home in the country. I stop by to check on the situation on my way to the office. I walk to the door wearing my grey wool, Sacks Fifth Avenue coat and matching tam, my hands clothed in black leather gloves. The lady of the house lets me in and we sit in her living room as she tells me of her husband who is out of work and the welfare relief jungle through which she is wading. As we talk of her lack of money to feed the animals and pay the electric bill, she sips coffee and smokes cigarettes, and I reflect on our cultural rules that say the poor are not deserving of such pleasures. At one moment our eyes meet with an understanding embrace, as she proudly shows me the second-hand Christmas decorations she has about the house. She says that she made her husband promise not to light the Christmas candles for fuel. I reflect on my own Waterford crystal decorations I set out only days before. We knowingly share an unspoken dream of making our houses into homes. I return later with dog, cat, and people food. . . . And so begins my uncanny exposure to poverty and the families who live on the "other side of the tracks."

Introduction

Women's Choices and the Risk of Poverty chronicles the lives of 47 women from Oklahoma and their experiences with being poor. Using qualitative and quantitative methods, the author examines the relationship between the age at which a woman first gives birth, her marital status then and later in life, and her corresponding risk for entering and exiting poverty. Five categories of women who cycle in and out of poverty are identified in the research—Welfare Dependent, Cyclers, Combiners, Temporary Poverty, and Self Sufficient. The author illustrates each type of poverty through insightful, sometimes witty and other times sad, quotes from the case studies and quantitative analysis. Utilizing these case studies, she examines many facets of women's experiences in poverty. These range from sexual activity, contraceptive practices, and intimate relationships to their struggles as the primary caretakers dealing with education, employment and the maze of government assistance.

Dr. Methvin finds that many women shift between welfare dependency and husband dependency because of occupational segregation, primary child rearing responsibilities and other cultural factors she explores in the book. The research describes the provocative relationships between low wages for females, their marriage and educational choices, the limited marriage pool for African American females, and the feminization of poverty. *Women's Choices and the Risk of Poverty* concludes with a discussion of how America's cultural rules and post–industrial economy contribute to the increasing feminization of poverty and the consequences of welfare reform for the many faces of poverty.

The royalties from *Women's Choices and the Risk of Poverty* are being designated to the easing of human and animal suffering through donations to Habitat for Humanity and Volunteers for Animal Protection.

Acknowledgments

I would like to acknowledge the support of my colleagues and others at Cameron University, particularly my students whose enthusiasm gave me energy when I needed it most; Research Center staff, especially Debbie Crossland and Donnie Hall; Computer Services; Foundation staff; and the faculty of West Hall who encouraged me and listened to ideas in the hallways during the months of writing and research. Sue Ellen Wilson, also of Cameron, tirelessly revised the manuscript—what will we do with our Tuesday evenings, Sue?. Troy Abell, Doctoral Chair, Betty Harris, Ross Hassig, Lesley Rankin-Hill, and Dee Ann Wenk of the University of Oklahoma provided guidance during the trial-by-fire doctoral process from which this manuscript resulted. My parents, Roy and Mary Warner, Aunt Nancy Tartaglia and late Uncle Bud taught me to believe in myself and were always there when I needed them. My friends, especially, Deanna Durbin, Lois Howell, Burl Haile, and Kate Held spent many hours listening to me as I sorted out the complexities of this research. I will never forget those talks among us. My family, Alan Morris and the animals, probably sacrificed the most. During the times when I was too tired or busy, their love and joy nourished my soul. Finally, I would like to thank the women whose lives are chronicled herein who opened up their lives and homes to me; my life is richer for having met them. I am indebted to each of you and I thank you for traveling part of the path with me. Many thanks,

Sharon

Women's Choices and
the Risk of Poverty

I
Overview of the Study

Poverty in Oklahoma

Today the female headed family is the most rapidly increasing type of family in American society. As illustrated in Table 1, such families in Oklahoma account for 41 percent of all African American, compared to 25 percent of all American Indian, 17 percent of Hispanic American, 14 percent of European American and 12 percent of Asian American households (Bureau of the Census: 1990b). The vast majority of these females are not widows, but women with children under 18 years old. A tripling in the number of divorces, a five-fold increase in the number of nonmarital pregnancies, and changes in the economic structure account, in large part, for the increases in female headed households with children.

Female headed families also represent the largest poor segment of Oklahoma, giving support to the increasing feminization of poverty that is occurring nationwide. In fact, such families in Oklahoma account for nearly three-fourths (72 percent) of all poor African American families and about one-half (46 percent and 51 percent) of all poor European American and American Indian families (Bureau of the Census: 1990b).

Poverty not only disproportionately affects women, it also disproportionately affects ethnic minorities, thus placing minority female headed families at greatest risk for poverty. To illustrate, in 1960 the average minority female headed family with children living in Oklahoma

3

earned $1,562 a year compared to $4,620 or one-third (34 percent) of what other families (urban and rural combined) earned. These 11,017 families represented 11 percent of all Oklahoma families but 24 percent of all minority families (Bureau of the Census: 1960b). By comparison, in 1990, there were 44,000 female headed families, representing 15 percent of all Oklahoma families. While much of the increase occurred among European Americans, female headed families by 1990 represented 41 percent (34 percent of those with children) of all African American families, a substantial larger percentage than for any other group.

As illustrated in Figure 1, the median income in Oklahoma for European American families in 1990 was $30,168 and for African American families, $18,511 (Bureau of the Census: 1990b). Female headed families earned considerably less. Among European Americans the average household income in 1990 was $12,021, which was just at the poverty threshold for a family of four in 1990. These families earned only 40 percent of what the average European American married couple family earned. African American female headed families fared the poorest. The average income in 1990 was only $7,345 for an African American female headed family with children. By comparison, these families earned 61 percent of European American female headed families, 40 percent of African American married couple families, and only about one-fourth (24 percent) of what European American married couple families earned. Minority female headed families are hit doubly hard because females earn less and minorities earn less (Figures 1 & 2). The reasons for the disparity in income are complex but the absence of a second income earner and occupational segregation by race and gender make it difficult for the majority of female headed families, and minority families in particular, to be economically well off.

Overview of the Study

Previous poverty research suggests that while the proportion of people below the poverty level remains fairly stable over time, the composition of the group is dynamic from year to year. Indeed, it has been suggested by some poverty researchers that from one-third to one-half of the impoverished population shifts from one income group to another in a given year (cf. Bane 1994; Bane and Ellwood 1983, 1984; Beeghley 1989; Duncan 1965; Ellwood 1993; Hill 1981). For example, in an analysis of ten years of the Panel Study of Income Dynamics (PSID) data on poverty, Bane and Ellwood found that the population who lives in poverty is quite heterogeneous and that, " . . . although many people have short spells of poverty, the few with long spells of poverty account for the bulk of all poverty and the bulk of the poor at any one point in time" (1983:2). By analogy, they point out that, "The proportion of chronically ill account for only a small fraction of all hospital admissions; however, because they stay for so long, they end up being a sizable part of the population in the hospital and they consume a sizable chunk of the hospital's beds and other resources" (1983:18).

In order to more fully understand the dynamic and heterogeneous composition of those in poverty, the present research incorporates a life span perspective. This study of poverty is based on oral interviews in the homes and neighborhoods of 47 women who, in many ways, are not unlike the women in the opening vignettes. These women who allowed me a glimpse into their life's tapestry also have personal dreams, meaningful treasures that make their houses "home," and concerns for the safety of their children who play outside. In this study on poverty, I investigate the life trajectories of four groups of females, defined by age and marital status at first birth, who delivered infants between 1988 and 1991 at Oklahoma Memorial Hospital (OMH) Women's Clinic and two Family Medicine Clinics in Oklahoma City, Oklahoma. The women are primarily low income patients who did not have private medical insurance approximately five years ago. At the time of their deliveries, all but two were receiving Medicaid to cover the cost of these pregnancies. While these births were not necessarily their first children, it was nevertheless the point at which they enrolled in the first phase of this study.

The focus of the present, or second, phase of the study is on the long-term effects of their age and marital status at the time of first giving birth, whenever that occurred. These effects are measured as potential risks that can influence a female's chance of entering poverty and the severity and duration of poverty she may experience over the life cycle. In addition to her age and marital status at the time of first birth, the research takes into account two additional factors, namely, the socioeconomic status of the parents and any changes in marital status subsequent to first giving birth. Specifically, there are four major hypotheses addressed in the study. The first considers the effects of parental background during the time of adolescence, or what is referred to in the model as stage one: the time before first birth. The hypothesis tested at stage one is whether those females whose teen years were spent in high risk environments are more likely to enter or to remain in poverty as adults and for longer periods. Based on the research by Hogan and Kitagawa (1983), high risk is defined as those whose parents were on government assistance, had a sister who had a child before age eighteen, or were from low income neighborhoods.

The second major hypothesis is tested at what is referred to as stage two in the model: the time of the first birth. At this stage the effects of the age at which a female first has a child, excluding adoptions, is studied. Following on the research of Furstenburg (1992), Lancaster (1986, 1989) and Upchurch and McCarthy (1990), the hypothesis predicts that females who have their first child at a younger age are more likely to enter poverty and to do so for more persistent periods than females who have their first child when older. The third major hypothesis is also tested at stage two. Following on the research of Geronimus (1991, 1992), Stack (1974) and Wilson (1987, 1991), it assesses the effects of marital status at the time or within three months of the first birth. This hypothesis predicts that females who are unmarried at the birth of their first child are more likely to enter poverty and to do so for more persistent periods than females who are married at the birth of their first child. In addition, the interaction between age and marital status is tested to determine if the proportion of females who have their first child at a younger age and are also unmarried at that time are at the greatest risk of entering poverty and remaining in poverty for the most persistent periods.

The final hypothesis is related to stage three in the model: the time subsequent to first birth. Following on the research of Arendall (1991), Bane (1994) and Bane and Ellwood (1983), it tests the effects of divorce for those females who ever married, be it at the time of the first birth or any time after. Specifically, the hypothesis predicts that females who marry but subsequently divorce are more likely to enter poverty and to do so for more persistent periods than those who remain married. Additionally, this stage compares those who married and divorced with those who never married.

Thus, the research incorporates a life span approach to the study of poverty using four independent and time-specific variables. A multivariate regression equation measures the effects of each variable separately and cumulatively to determine their separate and interactive effects as predictors of poverty. The sample is divided into four comparison groups that focus on the age and marital status at the time of the first birth. The groups are: (1) young (<18) and unmarried, (2) young and married, (3) older (18 and over) and unmarried, and (4) older and married.

This research is important for two reasons. First, it uses a time-specific life-cycle approach to examine the potential contribution of the age at which a female first gives birth and her marital status to the likelihood of entering and remaining in poverty. Second, it examines the extent to which other biological, cultural and societal factors can reduce or exasperate a woman's chances of becoming and remaining poor. The other risk factors examined include the onset of fertility, use of contraception, parental socioeconomic status, kinship support systems, educational attainment, availability of a marriage partner, the eligibility structure of government assistance, gender barriers in employment, ethnicity, and changes in cultural rules associated with divorce and marriage.

Table 1 Families in Poverty in Oklahoma: 1990

	African American	Asian American	European American	Hispanic American	Native American
All Families	30.6%	17.5%	10.2%	24.4%	24.0%
Rural Families	33.1%	22.9%	13.5%	28.6%	25.3%
Female Headed	*41.0%*	*12.3%*	*14.3%*	*17.0%*	*24.6%*
% of All **Poor** Families	*71.1%*	*26.5%*	*46.2%*	*39.2%*	*51.0%*
Female Headed <18	*33.5%*	*8.3%*	*10.0%*	*13.3%*	*18.1%*
% of All **Poor** Families	*66.5%*	*20.0%*	*41.1%*	*34.9%*	*44.0%*
All Individuals	42.8%	21.4%	12.8%	28.0%	28.1%
Rural Individuals	38.3%	17.3%	15.9%	34.0%	29.2%

Sources: Data for 1990 are from the 1990 Bureau of the Census, Census of Population, CP-Vol. 2, Part 38, *Social and Economic Characteristics*; 1990 Bureau of the Census, Current Population Reports, Series P-60, No. 175, *Poverty in the United States: 1991*; Bureau of the Census, Current Population Reports, Series P-60, No. 181, *Poverty in the United States: 1991*.

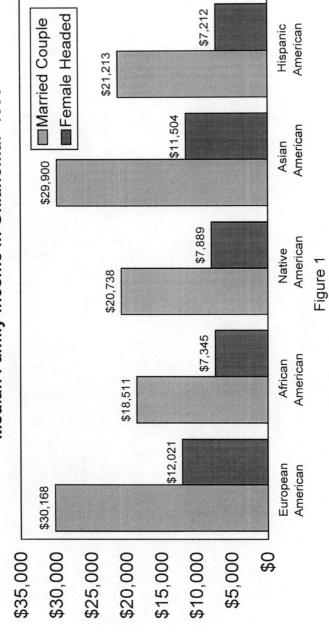

Annual Income

Median Family Income in Oklahoma: 1990

Figure 1

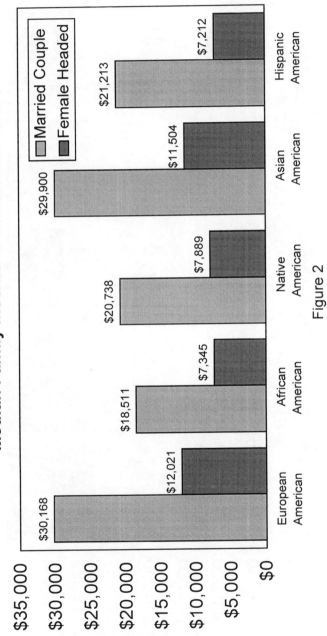

Figure 2

II
Literature Review

Introduction

The literature on poverty abounds. A recent data base search of the *Social Science Abstracts* revealed over 1,400 articles on poverty. Since time and space limit the amount of literature that can be reasonably reviewed, this review of the literature focuses on the research relevant to the four major hypotheses, specifically, parental socioeconomic status (SES), age at first birth, initial marital status at first birth, and ever married females who eventually divorce. Next, this section focuses on the literature relevant to the life cycle and adaptation approaches to the study of poverty. Finally, the significance of previous life span research on poverty is reviewed.

Theoretical Orientation

1. Adaptation Strategies Through the Life Cycle

Families grow through stages that are associated with cyclical changes in family tasks, reproductive and mate selection strategies and income. For example, as anthropologist Susan Greenhalgh in her study of poverty in Taiwan points out, " . . . a certain amount of economic inequality is purely demographic, stemming from the position of families in the developmental cycle" (1985:571). The importance of the life cycle/course approach to the study of poverty is critical to understanding the causes of poverty and the heterogeneous makeup of those who are poor.

Researchers such as Greenhalgh (1985); Stack (1974); Bane (1994); Bane
and Ellwood (1983); and Ellwood (1993) have noted that some poverty
is short-lived and will disappear automatically as families move up and
down through their developmental cycle. However, as Piven and Cloward
(1971); Wilson (1987, 1991); and Devine and Wright (1993) point out,
other causes of poverty are more persistent and intricately woven into the
structure of the larger cultural, political and economic systems.

The life cycle theoretical approach to the study of families originated
in the 1930s and is based on a time analysis. The importance of this
orientation lies in its attempt to account for changes in the family system
over time. This is important for the present research because, as biological
anthropologist Low notes, the costs and benefits of any reproductive
strategy, be it when to conceive or whom to marry, will differ for men and
women of different ages, occupations, wealth and health. These differing
costs and benefits will then lead to different adaptation patterns within
groups, depending on the composition of individuals and environmental
richness (1993).

Thus, the adaptive strategies that a female may employ at one stage
in the life cycle or in one environmental condition such as poverty, may
have a greater or lesser degree of associated costs than at a later stage in
the life cycle or under richer environmental circumstances. The
"reproductive value" (Low 1993) of the female, as an example, changes
over time and space depending on the point in the life cycle and her
environmental conditions. Women, whether in the United States or
elsewhere, make life choices that are constrained and sculpted by their
environmental, cultural, and structural conditions. (For example, see
Armelagos et al. (1972) for a treatment of this concept in relation to
restricted options among marginal groups such as the one under study in
this research.)

The choice-making process is more complex, however, because there
are tensions between varying options; while certain strategies may be
adaptive in the short term, they may have long-term costs (Mazess 1975).
For example, epidemiologist Geronimus (1991) and biosocial
anthropologist Lancaster (1986) suggest that among disadvantaged
populations, the higher incidence of early childbearing may be an
adaptive strategy that is a culturally patterned solution to the difficulty

and constraints of bearing and rearing healthy children in poverty. Factors such as the biological fitness of young females, lack of marriage partners, earlier incidence of deaths and availability of grandparent/kinship investment may explain why there is a greater incidence of early childbearing among disadvantaged populations. Geronimus develops the idea that this adaptive strategy may be the "culturally rational" thing to do for women in poverty because it optimizes the chances that dependents can be cared for (1991).

An important consideration is the extent to which a rational choice that is adaptive at one level or domain, such as the biological advantage conferred by early childbearing, may have associated costs in other areas. For example, to what extent does it create economic consequences or a diminished ability to attract a marriage partner. A second consideration is whether what is adaptive or most efficient in the short term may, in the long–term, be maladaptive. For example, while Geronimus (1991) suggests that early childbearing may be adaptive in the short term in that the females are more likely to deliver healthy infants, its costs in terms of subsequently completing an education and longer term economic consequences are raised by other poverty researchers (Upchurch and McCarthy 1990). The present study follows upon these previous studies and further assesses the potential costs and advantages of early childbearing and whether these women are more likely to end up in poverty and for longer periods than those who delay childbearing.

A final note on the concept of adaptation is the effect of the nonlocal economic and political structure on the group-level cultural rules, corresponding behavior, and subsequent physiological functioning of the individual. The introduction of the political economy perspective by Thomas, Gage and Little (1979) and others, recognizes that human behavior is a consequence of social relations and political relations that affect biological and group functioning. Often these social relations are unequal and are generated from beyond the boundaries of the local system by a political and economic system upon which the group becomes dependent.

These political and social relations have important consequences for the structure of government assistance requirements and their corresponding constraints on human behavior. The eligibility requirements create a circumstance wherein the adaptive choice, unless the male partner is economically stable, is for the female to remain unmarried. Lancaster (1989b:67) states, "The primary determinant of family formation and parental investment strategies should be the needs of women for access to resources to rear children . . . using this perspective, female headed, single parent households are viewed as created not by default of male interest, but rather by adaptations to particular distributions of social and physical resources in the environment." Whether females who remain unmarried and welfare dependent are financially better off than those who work or marry is addressed in the present research.

From the biocultural perspective, the social environment of poverty and its inequities is viewed as a perturbation or source of stress in the form of restricted opportunities that have physiological and behavioral consequences on the health and lifestyle of the group. System perturbations and the corresponding responses or adaptations, according to Mazess (1975), can occur at various levels or domains, specifically, genetic, morphological, physiological, psycho social, intragroup –household, and intergroup-community levels. For example, the development of fictive kin resource pools among poor female heads of households illustrates adaptation at the intergroup level, whereas, reliance by teen mothers on child care support from the extended family is a response at the intragroup or household level.

2. Accommodation versus Adaptation

Thomas notes that individuals swim upstream through a series of response strategies (currencies), each requiring greater resource costs relative to the derived benefit (Thomas, Winterhalder and McRae 1979; Thomas 1994). At each point an individual reaches a threshold where the less costly strategy is no longer able to maintain the system. At that point the individual must resort to strategies that are more costly and involve higher levels of irreversibility. At each stage, various adaptive units or domains compete for opportunities, such as the household with the community or state. The competitive tension between whether to marry or to receive Aid for Families with Dependent Children (AFDC) is but one example. Some choices may buffer or distribute the effects of the stressor. Another response strategy is to conform or accommodate to the external crisis, at least temporarily, until other options become available. Reliance on government assistance and maintaining a separate residence from the partner might be viewed as an example of an accommodation strategy. Finally, when the responses are not adequate, the system will become dysfunctional and fail to persist or significantly reorganize, what Thomas (1994) calls a system crash. Substance abuse, homelessness, prostitution and other traumas are examples of outcomes from such inadequate responses.

A biocultural and life cycle approach to studying poverty provides a model or framework through which the conditions, consequences, responses and corresponding outcomes of living in poverty can be viewed. In that sense it is a skeleton on which the observations in the field can be hung and arranged. It is a way of thinking about or structuring social phenomena. The validation of the appropriateness of the model depends upon the ability of the model to generate testable hypotheses about the relationships or interactions between the components, and the fruitfulness of the model in providing additional theoretical insight.

3. Decision Theory

Adaptation strategies over the life cycle are compatible with the economic theory of Rational Choice/Decision Theory in several important ways. It suggests that humans will act in accord with that which will maximize success for survival. Thus, it assumes there is a threshold at which, given our current structuring of governmental assistance, the rational choice would be for a female to remain unmarried and not to work outside the home. There are two other subjective utilities that must also figure into her decision, however, these being such moral economies of choice as self-concept and the cultural pressure to "earn a living" and secondly, such neighborhood economies of choice as safety for her children (Oliker 1994). Thus, what might seem the rational choice is weighted by other factors that are not purely economic nor necessarily the most optimum for ensuring fitness.

A second consideration is that rational choice or individual decision making is constrained by what are called structural effects, that is, the economy, age/sex ratios, political system, etc. So, while the rational choice might be to maintain certain behaviors, the political structure (also culturally sculpted) may require ideological and behavioral adjustments that might be in tension with or limit one's ability to initiate certain *rational* adaptive strategies. For example, it is probably adaptive to rear children in a two-parent home, if for no other reason than there are two persons to manage child care and other domestic as well as financial responsibilities. The political structure restricts this option because of AFDC and health care regulations. Medicaid and Aid for Families with Dependent Children are, for the most part, only available to women without husbands living in the same household. Thus, a matrilineal extended family system may become the most adaptive strategy among the poor, especially when, as Geronimus (1991), Stack (1974) and others suggest, the grandmother is young enough to provide child care and economic assistance.

4. Value Stretch
For those in poverty, fewer options are available and adaptive strategies are not only constrained but also eroded, leading to reliance on more costly and irreversible options and potential for diminished adaptive capacity over time, thereby leading to system crashes. The various response options humans select can then be called coping strategies but they have biological consequences (Thomas, Winterhalder, and McRae 1979). For example, a female receiving food stamp supplements may purchase poor nutritional quality foods because of the low price. However, its nutritional and caloric content may create physiological stressors such as obesity.

Cultural rules suggest that it is good to work and good to have a partner to assist in childbearing. However, among the poor both cultural rules have been constrained. The problem is as Merton (1938) suggests, the cultural rules or goals of marriage and work are held out to all, but the means to achieve them are not available to all. Thus, certain response strategies are opted for by those who cannot achieve the goal through the culturally approved means. Merton asserts that some retreat or completely reject the goal, such as the homeless, while others innovate and achieve the goal through non-legitimate means such as crime. However, the most interesting response strategy is among those who modify the goal to one that is more achievable, such as can be seen among disadvantaged or young teens who have limited marriage opportunities when pregnant.

This concept is expanded on by Kohn (1977) and referred to as "value stretch." A value stretch is likely to occur if the current cultural rule is unachievable; it is then modified. So teens who would like to marry and raise a family but do not have stable employment, stretch the rule to having a child and maintaining an intimate partnership, but not marrying. Indirect support is found by Hogan and Kitagawa (1983:84) who reported that 57 percent of teens in high risk environments expected to become parents, on the average, two years before being married. On the other hand, only 4 percent of those in low risk environments expected to do so.

In conclusion, a life cycle and bioculutral approach to the study of poverty enables one to examine the complex relationship between the individual/behavioral level, the environment, the political/economic level and the cultural fabric. Viewing poverty within a life cycle context likewise permits an evaluation of the dynamic nature of poverty and its relationship to changes in jobs, family structure and health. This research proposes that there are four major life circumstances that will influence a female's chances of entering poverty, namely, her environment while growing up, the age and marital status as she first begins to parent, and changes in marital status later in life. The next section discusses the pertinent literature related to each of these life circumstances.

Hypothesis One: Parental Socioeconomic Status

1. Occupational Mobility and Parental SES
The impact of parent's economic position on their offspring's life opportunities has been extensively studied. Sociologists such as Macionis suggest, "Nothing affects social standing in the United States as much as our birth into a particular family. Being born into privilege or poverty sets the stage for our future schooling, occupation and income" (1995:270). There is some vertical mobility, however, between social classes in spite of the inequality in opportunity conferred by parental SES.

De Jong, Brawer and Robin (1971) first studied intergenerational mobility for women, but their research did not indicate whether the occupation was the female's first or a later job (Kerbo 1996). A more precise study by Hauser and Featherman (1977) found that women are concentrated in lower nonmanual positions regardless of whether their fathers are in higher or lower occupational positions. In other words, the female is concentrated in a low paying clerical or retail position regardless of parental SES. An understanding of labor market segmentation by gender is important for the present research. Even when a female is able to work full-time and raise a family, she is less likely than her male educational counterpart to find a position that pays above $6.00 per hour. Lyon et al. (1982) in an analysis of the National Longitudinal Survey found " . . . evidence of sexual discrimination in the allocation of occupational rewards" (1982:534). With comparable education assets, they make on the average 30 percent less than males. On the other hand, Abell (1979) and Lyon et al. (1982) note that occupational stratification is multidimensional. For females, occupational status does not translate into economic status. Moreover, the female rarely receives the benefits that are associated with unionized, trade employment for males. Abell found that the low wage positions into which females tend to be segregated have greater occupational prestige than men's occupations, but that did not correspond with economic remuneration (1979). Thus, an important distinction should be made between the economic rewards versus social status associated with an occupation.

In addition to occupational stratification by gender, one must also consider stratification by ethnicity. To what degree do African American mobility patterns resemble those of the general population? When comparing outflow data for lower manual occupations in 1962, Kerbo (1996) found a more rigid degree of intergenerational class inheritance (70 percent) for African American males as compared to 43 percent for all groups combined. In fact only 8.3 percent of African American sons moved upward from their father's lower nonmanual position as compared to 43.1 percent of the general population. By 1973 there was a 30 percent improvement in the inheritance of upper nonmanual positions. However, for those African Americans in nonmanual positions in 1973, 61 percent inherited their father's class as compared to 40 percent of the general population. Unfortunately, this study did not include an analysis of mobility patterns for African American females (Kerbo 1996).

Only 13.3 percent of the African American sons in 1962 who had fathers with upper nonmanual positions were able to attain such positions as compared to 57 percent of the general population (Kerbo 1996). In fact, 63 percent of African American males whose fathers held upper nonmanual positions moved down to lower manual positions. By 1973 there was an improvement, but still only about half of those whose fathers had upper nonmanual positions were able to inherit this occupational class. Occupational stratification by gender and ethnicity is also reviewed in the present study.

2. Labor Market Segmentation

In addition to gender and ethnic stratification in the labor market, segmentation within the same occupation can occur between market sectors. One of the key situational effects this creates is that of a dual economy, meaning that certain industries and large corporations are found in the core industrial areas and those employed in the core earn more than those with comparable jobs in small scale, nonunion businesses in the periphery. An example is the unionized trade of the United Mine Workers of America whose collective bargaining power produces high wages for its members versus the nonlegal immigrant mine workers substandard wages.

A corollary is that industrialization occurs unevenly within the United States and within each region, state and city. So, for example, in Oklahoma there are a larger number of poor and a lower median income than found nationwide, or in the Northeast economic corridor. The contraction of the manufacturing sector and the urban flight has disproportionately affected different geographic areas within and between states. In addition, central city communities have changed as industries and population have shifted to the suburbs. Prior to 1960, the central cities exhibited different features of social organization and a vertical integration of different segments of the population, because of residential segregation by ethnicity. All classes of African American, Hispanic and other minority families lived in the same community and sent their children to the same schools and attended the same community events;

whereas, today the same central city communities are almost all occupied by the most disadvantaged segments of all ethnic groups. These communities are heterogenous groups with one thing in common—the people who live there interact in the same depressed community as part of the U.S. population that has become increasingly isolated socially and economically from mainstream patterns and norms of behavior. (See Devine and Wright (1993) for a thorough discussion of this view.)

Labor market and residential segmentation have had serious consequences for the urban poor. For example, unemployment ratios of African American to European American did not reach 2:1 until 1954. Before that there was actually greater African American employment, although it was primarily in the lowest wage sector. Unemployment ratios have remained at above 2:1 every year since, and are the highest in the south and southwest regions of the U.S. (Devine and Wright 1993). Irrespective of the region, unemployment rates within the central cities, especially among young minorities, are five times higher than elsewhere and can reach as high as 70 percent among prime marriage-age males (Wilson 1987, 1991).

The age structure of the urban poor population is also changing. In the nation's central cities in 1977, the overall ethnic makeup was 30 percent European Americans, 24 percent African Americans, and 22 percent Hispanics. However, the number of central city African Americans aged fourteen to twenty-four rose 78 percent from 1960 to 1970 as compared to an increase of only 23 percent for European Americans (Wilson 1987). In short, much of what has gone awry in inner cities is affected by the sheer increase in the number of young people, especially young minorities, the contraction of the manual labor market and the geographic labor market segmentation.

3. The Relationship Between Age at First Birth and Parental SES

An important consideration of the effects of parental socioeconomic status concerns the age at which a female first gives birth. In a study noted earlier, drawing upon data from Chicago, Hogan and Kitagawa (1985) estimated that 57 percent of teens from high risk social environments will become pregnant by age eighteen as compared to only 9 percent of teens from low risk social environments. They define a high risk environment as having a low parental economic status, living in inner-city neighborhoods, living in a female headed family, having five or more siblings, having a sister who is a teen mother, and having loose parental supervision (1985). The present research likewise compares the age at which first birth occurs with the environment in which the female was living as a teen.

Parental SES may also affect marital status at the time of first birth. Hogan and Kitagawa (1983) further report that while African American teens expect to become parents at roughly the same time as European American teens, they do not expect to marry until a later age. When adjusted for social class, expected age specific rates of parenthood for African Americans is only 2 percent lower than for European Americans but expected age specific rates for marriage are 36 percent lower.

4. Educational Attainment and Parental SES
A final consideration is the effect of parental SES on education. Education is the variable most closely associated with an increase in economic status and is directly influenced by one's parent's socioeconomic status. Being born middle class is closely correlated with the likelihood of attending college. And those who finish college have a greater occupational advantage over those who do not. IQ has little to do with whether you attend college. Only about 45 percent of IQ is biologically determined. Nevertheless, 80 percent of middle class children, but only 20 percent of lower class children attend college irrespective of IQ. Over 90 percent of middle class children with high IQ attend college, but only around 40 percent of lower class children with high IQ's attend. Sewell and Shah (1968) found, when looking at the other end of the intelligence rank, that among those in the higher social classes approximately 58 percent of those with low IQ attend college, whereas only 9.3 percent of those with low IQ from lower social classes attend (in Kerbo 1996:375).

What really counts, of course, is who completes college among those who manage to enter. Kaplan and Lancaster (1995) make the important point that college retention rates will also vary by social class. She notes, "The acquisition of many skills that bring economic return is dependent upon the base of precedent skills in which they are built . . . This is especially evident in university education in which success and drop out rates appear to be well predicted by the base of skills established in high school" (1995:128).

College completion rates are sensitive to ethnicity, gender and economic background. As can be seen in Figure 3, according to the 1990 census data for Oklahoma, for all age groups combined, approximately 22 percent of European American males attained a Bachelors Degree, whereas only 12 percent of African American males did so. Among females, 16 percent of European Americans compared to 12 percent of African Americans obtained a Bachelor's degree[1] (Bureau of the Census: 1990b).

Hypothesis Two: Age at First Birth

1. Increasing Nonmarital Birth Rates

While teen birth rates have slightly declined, nonmarital pregnancy rates have not (Jones et al. 1991). This difference can be accounted for in several ways. First, teen birth rates have declined because birth control measures are more readily available. However, those teens who do give birth are marrying less frequently (addressed more fully in the next section) and others who become pregnant are aborting or adopting out instead of rearing the children. As of 1973 abortions were legally available. The rate for teens rose to 43 abortions per 1000 teens by 1980 and has stabilized at that level (Jones et al. 1991). One reason for the decline in birth, but not pregnancy rates for teens, is the access to legal abortion. Restricted access and increasingly restrictive cultural rules concerning abortion will consequently affect teen birth rates. Abortions have been and will always be available to those with money. Money buys options. Thus, when our nation discusses restricting abortion, the restrictions most adversely impact those who are poor and those who are young because of the limited private finances and health coverage available to them.

While nonmarital pregnancy rates of teens have increased, part of the increase is an artificial inflation due to the decline in marital birth rates for all age groups including teens (Wilson 1987:66-67). In fact, the marital birth rate has steadily declined by roughly half for African Americans and by 40 percent for European Americans. Nevertheless, the ratio of nonmarital births to marital births has increased by a factor of four (quadrupled) for European American and a rate of one-fourth (25 percent) for African Americans since 1960. While the nonmarital birth rate for European Americans has grown more rapidly, the total numbers for African Americans far exceeds that of European Americans (Wilson 1987).

For the nation in 1982, 57 percent of births to African Americans and 12 percent of births to European Americans age 15 to 19 were to unmarried teens, a ratio of nearly 5:1. However, these figures incorporate all teens, including those 18 to 19 year olds. The state level data for Oklahoma school age pregnancies (meaning to those ages 17 or younger) is even more revealing. The Department of Health found in 1992, that 97 percent of African American teens who gave birth between the ages of 15 to 17 were unmarried while 65 percent of their European American counterparts were (Personal Communication: Oklahoma State Department of Health: Oklahoma Prams-Gram Survey Data).

These figures reveal two important trends. First, when looking only at school age pregnancies instead of all teen pregnancies, the number of females who do not marry skyrockets. Second, the difference of 32 percent in marital rates between ethnic groups suggests that different behavioral and economic factors may be occurring between European and African American teens.

2. Biological Factors Associated with Age at First Birth

There are numerous biological, cultural and economic factors that may be associated with when a female begins to parent, regardless of her marital status. For example, Frisch's (1978) critical fat hypothesis states, " . . . that women will not ovulate until adequate lower body fat stores are deposited to permit a women to lactate for a year or more without having to increase her prepregnancy caloric intake" (in Lancaster 1986:26). He further states that sedentism combined with high and more adequate caloric and nutritional intake have created earlier fertility in industrial societies. The earlier onset of fertility is not limited to the United States but reflects a cross-cultural trend. Among the Bushmen of the Kalahari

Desert in South Africa, Frisch notes that while menses begins at about 16.5, young women do not conceive until about three years later. Frisch (1978) notes that with industrialization the onset age of menses declines. This may reflect improvements in nutrition that allow the adequate lower body fat accumulation for lactation during pregnancy, thereby allowing for earlier onset of fertility. This subsequently creates an earlier biological onset of menarche, thereby creating an earlier opportunity for pregnancy before adolescents have acquired the cultural and economic skills needed for parenting in a post-industrial society (in Lancaster 1986). This phenomenon illustrates the provocative question being explored by biocultural anthropologists regarding the degree to which culture—in this instance, industrialization—may be impairing biology (cf. Thomas 1994). A second related question of interest is whether those females with a greater accumulation of lower body fat might conceive sooner than other females who begin to engage in sexual activity at the same time.

3. Ideological and Behavioral Issues Associated with Age at First Birth
Secondly, there are ideological and behavioral issues associated with teen pregnancy, including the relationship between peer pressure and other learning factors in high–risk environments, that may account for part of the higher incidence of pregnancy among some teens. One important factor is that the culturally normative age at which we marry in the U.S. has been changing. Eshleman points out that " . . . the median age at which people first marry, as well as the age difference between partners, have changed considerably since the turn of the century" (1994:241-242). He notes that since 1956, the median age for marriage has increased from an all–time low of 22.5 and 20.1 for males and females respectively; whereas, today there has been a median increase of four years for males (26.5) and 4.3 years for females (24.4). Consequently, there is a longer time period between when a female is sexually receptive and when there is a culturally approved means for being sexually active, thereby creating a longer period of time during which nonmarital pregnancy can occur.

Secondly, there are changing normative views regarding adolescence and sexuality today. Both have greater permissiveness than previously in our society. Rodgers and Rowe (1993) make the point that sexuality is one of many transitional behaviors for adolescents. Just at the time that our hormonally driven biological desire and cultural pressure (social contagion) to mate is increasing, parental control is diminishing; teens have the opportunity to achieve some degree of independence through automobiles, unchaperoned dating, etc. In many cultural contexts, such as among Muslims, such practices are not the case (Jones et al. 1991). In our society, however, sexual behavior which initially is disapproved of can eventually become normative and a status-related behavior for the subgroup of youth.

A final cultural/behavioral issue associated with teen pregnancy is the availability of contraception. We simply do not have a safe, easy to use contraceptive practice available that appeals to a teen. It is unrealistic to expect most adults to remember to take a series of antibiotics ten days in a row without missing one dose. Likewise, it is unrealistic to think a teen will remember to take a birth control pill consistently. The use of condoms is gradually spreading because of the massive campaign to curtail AIDS. And certainly the variety of interesting condoms now becoming available holds tremendous promise for their appeal to teens. Nevertheless, studies (e.g. Williams and Kornblum 1991) show that most teens do not consistently use condoms or any other form of contraception. Until a form of safe, cheap, and easy to use contraception, such as the morning-after-pill, is part of our cultural norms, teen contraceptive use will likely be sporadic. Contraceptive practice is also addressed in the present study.

Finally, the literature suggests that cultural values regarding sexual activity today are different than that of the 1950s and 60s. The previous practice was limited to what is commonly called engagement coitus (e.g. Williams and Kornblum 1991). Today sexual activity trends before marriage will likely involve multiple partners. Part of the crucial debate presently between liberals and conservatives is whether our goal should be to curtail pregnancy, births, or sexual activity. These are often lumped together and, yet they require vastly different measures and are qualitatively different issues that reflect differing cultural rules.

4. Societal or Structural Factors Associated with Age at First Birth
The third area which influences the age of first birth is that of societal or structural issues such as the relationship between educational attainment and employment opportunities. Previous research has found that those who have babies and have not finished high school are less likely to complete school (Furstenburg 1991). Of those who leave school, some researchers suggest that as many as 50 to 75 percent never return. Upchurch and McCarthy (1990) note that the high school completion rate for all teens is around 90 percent; whereas for those who get pregnant, it is about 50 percent. In a study by Hoffman, Foster, and Furstenburg (1991) using sister pairs, they show that teen mothers are at a considerable disadvantage. They estimate that were teen mothers to delay their first birth to the age of their sister's first birth, high school completion rates would increase from 54 percent to 72 percent.

However, Furstenburg (1992) and Nord et al. (1992) make an important point; it is uncertain whether those students who do not finish high school would have dropped out anyway. A final point made by Upchurch and McCarthy (1990), and one that is addressed in the present research, is that some who never complete high school, estimated as high as 25 percent, have dropped out of school before ever becoming pregnant. For some teens, getting pregnant is just one more factor in a downward spiral that has already begun.

There are numerous programs available to assist teens in remaining in school during and after having a baby. Furstenburg (1991, 1992); Geronimus (1991); Nord et al. (1992); and Upchurch and McCarthy (1990) concur that the high school completion rate for teens with babies has grown more quickly than for the general teen population, suggesting that homebound and other programs for teens who are pregnant are having an impact. The effects of teen versus later births on educational attainment as well as the impact of educational programs for teen mothers are addressed in the present study.

Perhaps even more important than high school completion is whether the age at which a female first gives birth affects the likelihood that she will attend college, given that greater amounts of education are needed in order to compete successfully in a post–industrial economy. The literature (e.g. Furstenburg 1992) suggests that even those teen mothers who do receive high school diplomas are less likely to attend college than those who delay childbearing. In Furstenburg's (1991) study of sisters, he estimates that if sisters having teen births had delayed the age of first birth, college attendance would likely have risen from 14 to 26 percent.

What seems to be an important factor in determining a teen mother's ability to remain in school is whether a support group, especially kinship, is available to assist with child care and living arrangements during the school completion period. Another factor is the birth spacing between the first and second child. This is because many teens are able to manage juggling the demands of school, child care, work, etc. with one child, but parental investment strategies require additional energy and greater costs with the introduction of a second offspring. A final consideration is that even when the needed assistance is available, Williams and Kornblum (1991) note that returning to school takes on less importance if it will not definitely lead to a job that pays enough to cover both living costs and child care.

High teen pregnancy rates cross-culturally have been correlated with the degree of religiosity in the country, availability and easy access to contraception, and degree of school sex education. According to Jones et al. (1991), the U.S. has a far higher pregnancy rate than many industrialized nations. Our rate is twice as high as that of Canada, France, England, and three times as high as Sweden and the Netherlands. In addition, we have the highest abortion rates of all these countries. In other instances, where other pregnancy rates are high, the outcomes differ from those in the U.S. On the Kibbutzim in Israel, 42 percent of teens report having sexual intercourse, usually in the course of a stable relationship; 30 percent of females report using contraception (Kaffman 1977). While sexual sanctions are generally not imposed in the Kibbutz, the nonmarital pregnancy rates are far lower than in the U.S. This is because marriage for pregnant teens is generally the norm; whereas the cultural rules regarding marriage for pregnant teens in the U.S. have become more relaxed. Williams and Kornblum (1991) suggest that many teens think of the baby almost as a doll or as someone to love. They refer to some teens as "Sneaker Mothers," for whom sex is part of a recreational pattern that includes television, consuming vast quantities of pizza and soda, recreational drugs and booze, and making love with your man. This attitude toward sex is addressed in the present study.

A final consideration regarding the age of first birth is the number of additional children the female has subsequent to her first, and the spacing between those children. Smith (1992) discusses birth spacing as a cross cultural parental investment strategy. Demographic changes over the last few hundred years have revolutionized women's lives much more than they have men's. With a longer life expectancy and fewer pregnancies—and those occurring within a truncated reproductive span—a woman of around forty, if she begins her childbearing early, has probably raised her children and has almost another forty years to live. Only one in two women born in 1750 lived to age fifteen and one in three reached age fifty (Segalen 1988). Under such reproductive circumstances, early childbearing and short intervals between births may allow the woman to complete her childbearing, acquire a college education, and be vested in a corporation before retirement age. In fact, the average student age at Cameron University in Oklahoma, a regional university at which I am employed, is 27, and in the social sciences, it is 33.6.

In preindustrial times a female, during her ten to fifteen childbearing years, could expect to have five to six children with four surviving. With the dramatic reduction in death rates and greater life expectancy rates, today's female fecundity rate could potentially produce 12.3 children (Segalen 1988:60). However, much of the decline in household size in modern families has been attributed to women having fewer babies rather than reaching their full fertility potential. Lancaster and Hamburg (1986) make the point that today it makes sense from a biological standpoint to invest in fewer children because their chances of surviving to adulthood are much higher and because the period of dependency has been extended through high school and even college. One important question for predicting poverty is the number and spacing of dependents, both in order to maximize parental investment in the offspring and to optimize the parent's economic opportunities. Once again these demographic changes raise the question as to whether culture may be impairing biology. For example, under certain circumstances, cultural rules create the expectation that a female who becomes involved with a new partner produce additional offspring spaced ten or more years after her first child (children), yet adequate resources to invest in the second set of offspring may be lacking. In such cases, the childbearing years are greatly expanded making a return to college or higher occupational achievement, while not impossible, more difficult because of two distinct periods of dependent children for which to care.

The literature also suggests that the number of children a female bears differs by ethnicity as well her fecundity potential. For example, in every year studied by Kain (1990) since 1920, the first year African American rates for females were recorded, the fertility rates for African Americans have been consistently higher than for European Americans. In Carol Stack's (1974) study of people in the Flats, she found that among the predominantly African American poor, babies were conceived at very young ages and were highly valued. This was so regardless of whether a father was part of the household or not. In fact, Stack found that commonly a female would not marry or leave her natal home until her second pregnancy.

Of debate is whether this practice is due to differences in onset of menarche, cultural rules, or economic factors. One aspect of the debate infers that the maternal-child bond is higher than the two-parent bond because of the nature of the African American family structure under historic discrimination and impoverished conditions. Another aspect of the debate says that the higher incidence of nonmarital births for African Americans is a result of higher rates of male unemployment and conditions of government resources which make the mother-child bond the most rational adaptation. When adjusted for social class, nonmarital pregnancy rates even out across ethnic boundaries, suggesting that environmental conditions related to poverty are the determining factors. A second source of support for this view is that the incidence of nonmarital, early child rearing is growing more rapidly among European Americans who have not experienced the historic discrimination of African Americans, but are today living in poverty (Wilson 1987).

According to the National Center for Health Statistics (in Wilson 1987), fertility rates for both married and nonmarried females have declined since 1960, except among nonmarried females ages fifteen to nineteen. For example, in 1980, 68 percent of births to African American females ages fifteen to twenty-four were to unmarried females as compared to 41 percent in 1955. Additionally, a recent survey asserts that almost 30 percent of all unmarried African American females have given birth before the age of twenty (Wilson 1991). Finally, Wilson reports that almost 82 percent of premarital pregnancies to females ages 15 to 19 are reported as unwanted. But Ellwood (1993); Furstenburg(1992), Williams and Kornblum (1991) and others note, it is not that they are unwanted, it is just that they are not sufficiently unwanted—so as to prevent pregnancy. This attitude toward teen pregnancy is addressed in the present study.

As noted above, the rate of nonmarital births for teens is not falling as they are for older women. Almost 40 percent of all nonmarital births are to women under age 20 (Wilson 1987). However, Hogan and Kitagawa (1985) note that among African American teenagers, especially in high risk environments, fewer pregnancies are reported as unwanted. Thus, in high risk environments where options are limited, group variations in attitudes and behavior may reflect variations in group access to channels of privilege and influence. Kohns suggests that this may be in part because of the concept of value stretching discussed earlier. Individuals living in disadvantaged situations often adjust their attitudes, beliefs, and values to account for their bleak prospects. In other words, when the mainstream values cannot be achieved, values more readily achievable evolve—such as having a baby to gain adult status and have unconditional love. For example, a child is a symbol of the fact that the female is now a woman and the status she may gain from having something of her own (Williams and Kornblum 1991). This attitude toward pregnancy is addressed in the present study.

Hypothesis Three: Marital Status at First Birth

1. Differential Male Marriage Pool

Wilson (1987, 1991) and others (e.g. Levine 1991) argue that one of the reasons for the increase in birth rates among never married females, especially among African Americans, is a result of increasing unemployment rates among those of prime marriageable age. These researchers go on to state that because of economic instability, high incarceration rates, and homicidal deaths, coupled with the cultural rules of homogamy and hypergamy, there are fewer men available in the "male marriageable pool"—meaning those men who are young, economically stable, and can support a family at a level above poverty. The lack of opportunities for marriage, especially among African American women, is also addressed in the present study.

Wilson (1987) cites the differentially shrinking labor force participation rates as evidence that fewer African American males are available to marry. While labor force participation among European American men ages 24 and under actually increased between 1970 and 1982, the patterns are different for African Americans in the same age category. For them it has declined from 84 percent in 1940 to only 64 percent in 1980. Interestingly, the employment contraction is among the young. Among older African American males the pattern differs; it parallels their European American age cohort.

Wilson (1987, 1991) attributes the increasing unemployment among young males without college degrees to the labor force segmentation and contraction of the manufacturing sector, discussed earlier, that adversely affected different segments of the population and geographic regions. To illustrate, between 1947 and 1972, the central cities of the 33 most populous metropolitan areas lost 880,000 manufacturing jobs, while manufacturing employment in the suburbs grew by 2.5 million. The central cities lost 867,000 jobs in retail and wholesale jobs at the same time that their suburbs gained millions of such positions. The decline in blue collar employment in the central city has been partly offset by expansion in knowledge intensive fields such as advertising and finance, but the new labor force positions require training at the post-high school level.

In conclusion, Wilson finds that while changes in the ratios of employed men to women among European Americans have been minimal, the ratios for African Americans have declined substantially in all regions of the country except the west. Wilson considers the increasing rate of joblessness to be a major factor in the rise of African American single mothers and female households. As noted above, the male marriage pool index (MMPI) imbalance is also compounded by the high homicide and incarceration rates, as well as cultural rules of who is a favored marriage partner, making the proportion of males in the "MMPI" even lower. The net result is a 41 percent increase in the number of African American children growing up in fatherless families since the 1970's. Most of the increase is from mothers who have never been married (Bane and Ellwood 1984:3). Moreover, the majority of these women already lived below the poverty level before becoming female householders. In Oklahoma, these women comprise 70 percent of all poor African Americans (Bureau of the Census: 1990b).

Lancaster (1989) concurs with Wilson's assessment. She states:

> We can predict the rate of facultative polyandry (serial male partners for offspring) and women as heads of households to remain stable or increase as long as men do not have predictable and sufficient access to those resources valued by women for reproduction. . . . the facultative polyandry rate has been driven by two factors: the creation of a large pool of underemployed males because of the precipitous drop in demand for unskilled labor, and the removal of large numbers of men from the potential marriage pool by jail, military service, drug addiction, and higher death rates from violence and risk taking (1989b:69).

According to Wilson (1987), one-quarter of all African American births in 1965 occurred outside of marriage, but by 1980, they had more than doubled to 57 percent. This corresponds with the rise in female headed families. In 1965, only one-quarter of African American households were female headed, but by 1980 this figure had risen to 43 percent. As mentioned before, there is a direct correlation between female headship and economic hardship. Nationally, in 1959 only 30 percent of all poor African American families were female headed, but by 1978, this figure had increased to 74 percent of all poor African American families.

These are the faces for whom Affirmative Action policies have had little impact because the opportunities they offer are not within their reach. What good is equal opportunity if one does not have the requisite education, child care or transportation by which to take advantage of the opportunities? Some suggest that there has been a "creaming" process in the sense that those with the greatest economic, educational and social resources among the less advantaged are the ones which are actually tapped for better paying jobs and higher educational opportunities, leaving those left behind concentrated in a tangled web of poverty, crime, and unemployment (Levine 1991).

Moynihan, in the 1960s, felt that the cumulative effects of discrimination made it almost impossible for many African Americans to take advantage of the opportunities provided by Civil Rights legislation. Devine and Wright (1993); Brooks (1990); and others concur, stating that there has been a bipolar class effect in which those African Americans who lack the requisite education and job skills have been unable to escape the effects of historic discrimination.

Murray (1984), in *Losing Ground*, argues that welfare is the fundamental cause of the disintegration of the African American family. He concludes that by 1970, the welfare package exceeded what a minimum wage earning family could bring in. Therefore, a couple's rational choice, precluding moral economies and cultural rules to the contrary, will be to cohabitate. Others have argued that these trends in benefits have reversed themselves and Greenstein (1985), in a rebuttal to Murray (1984), suggests that minimum wage and government transfers taken together today are around one-third higher than welfare benefits. Ellwood, (1993) disagrees, stating that wages must exceed $8.00 per hour to accrue a relative advantage over welfare benefits. Clearly then, the relationship between wages, welfare benefits and the choices women make is not a simple one. Government assistance benefits are but one factor in the increase in female headed families and their corresponding relationship to poverty. The cultural materialist's concept of infrastructure provides a useful way of thinking about the above discussion of the relationship between production and reproduction. Many of the factors are interrelated behavioral, ideological and structural components of United States culture.

2. Demographic and Cultural Factors in Relation to Marital Status

Demographic factors are another reason for the increased numbers of women who are not marrying. The age/sex structure of the United States has changed and is part of the problem associated with finding a marriage partner. In 1960 only 36 percent of African American and 34 percent of

European American females were between the ages of fifteen and twenty-four. However, by 1975 that proportion had increased by 10 percent for African American females and by 8 percent for European American females. Importantly, these changes in the age structure increased the prime age marriage group and the proportion of births occurring to young females (Wilson 1987:68-70).

Ideological and behavioral factors are a second consideration. Cultural expectations are both sculpted and constrained by the political economy in which they are nested. First, we have a cultural rule of hypergamy: females tend to marry up in our society, be it by age or class standing. Thus, a female's cultural expectation is that the male tends to be older and financially established (Veevers 1988). This makes sense in light of male/female differences in parental investment strategies. Lancaster (1986, 1989), for example, suggests that because a female has to invest considerable effort over a long period of time in one offspring, her reproductive strategy is to mate with a male who can provide the best productive resources to see the offspring through the long period of dependency. On the other hand, the male expends little reproductive effort in one offspring; therefore, his most successful strategy is to invest in as many offspring as possible to achieve the best or "fittest" offspring from the group of mates. These biological drives are filtered through cultural rules in our society that say a preferred mate for a female is one who is financially able to provide for her during childbearing and the offspring during the long dependent childrearing period. Whereas, the preferred mate for the male is one who is younger, can bear healthy children, and is visually attractive.

Sutherland's Differential Association Theory (in Macionis 1995) suggests that as we become inculcated in our particular society, we are differentially exposed to both normative cultural rules and deviant behavior. If we are more frequently exposed to a particular behavior, we become habituated to it as normative whether the exposure is through parental, peer, or media influences. This exemplifies how cultural rules that govern behavior may vary by group and how they are selectively filtered and interpreted by individuals in society. An example stated earlier is the findings by Hogan and Kitagawa (1983) showing that teens in low resource environments commonly expect to become parents at roughly the same time as others but do not expect to marry until much later.

3. Government Entitlement as Father

Anthropologist Carol Stack (1974) argues that the position of the male is weakened in poor families because the social welfare benefit system strongly rewards families in which there is only one adult present, thus creating a marriage disincentive. The high numbers of single parents in the study sample compared with the general population is studied in relation to the position of the male in the post-industrial poor family. Regulations regarding the distribution of government subsidies are an example of how cultural notions of who is *deserving* sculpt and regulate the distribution of government subsidies, which can in turn shape family formation practices. The cultural dimensions of hunger, eating and assistance programs mirror the prevailing cultural notions about the poor and poverty (Fitchen 1988). Stack also points out that even for those poor who do marry, household composition is quite vulnerable. Household composition may change and either expand or contract with the loss of a job, the beginning or end of a sexual relationship, the frequent evictions or condemnations of one's residence, competing kinship obligations, illnesses and deaths (Stack 1974).

4. Differences in Marital Status by Ethnicity

Research by Bane 1994; Bane and Ellwood 1983, 1984; and Ellwood 1993 distinguished that the route to a female headed family differs between ethnic groups. They state that among European Americans the rise in the proportion of nonmarried mothers is mainly because of increases in separation and divorce; whereas, among African American mothers it is a result of a decrease in marriage rates, coupled with an increase in fertility among never married women. Importantly, these differences may have consequences for the respective duration of poverty cycles for each ethnic group.

One-half of all European American female heads are divorced and one-fourth are separated. Among African Americans the circumstances are reversed; only 20 percent have been divorced; whereas, 50 percent have never been married. This has far-reaching consequences for the children of America. For example, in 1982 the percentage of African American children living with both parents had dipped to 43 percent, about half of the number of European American children in two-parent families. By the time children born into "subfamilies" (as defined by the US Bureau of the Census) reach age six, two-thirds will have moved into different living arrangements. But, among African Americans, two-thirds of the moves are into female headed households, while among European American, two-thirds are into two-parent families either through marriage or remarriage (Bane and Ellwood 1984).

One of the reasons for the different trajectories between the two ethnic groups may be because of structural changes in labor force participation addressed by Wilson and Lancaster above. African Americans, especially young males are dropping out of the labor force in significant numbers. By 1984, only 58 percent of all African American young adult males were employed. Importantly, only 34 percent of those eighteen to nineteen were employed compared to 70 percent of European American males in the same age group. Only 16 percent of African American males ages sixteen to seventeen were employed compared to 47 percent of European American males in the respective age group (Wilson 1987).

Those ages sixteen to nineteen are the very age group in which pregnancy without corresponding marriage is increasing. It is also the very age group that is at highest risk for entering and remaining in poverty, and is the focus of the present longitudinal study. The poverty rate is 32 percent for all persons ages fifteen to twenty-four, while only seven percent for those age forty-five to fifty-four (Wilson 1991). This suggests that those in poverty today are not only disproportionately never married or divorced female headed households, and disproportionately non-European American, but also disproportionately young.

The causes of the rise in female householders are multifaceted. The increase in the proportion of extramarital births could be mainly a function of the increasing difficulty of finding a marriage partner with stable employment, or of changes in the social values regarding nonmarital births, or of the increased economic independence afforded women by the availability of income transfers by the government. The rapid increase in female headship has created fear in the American public for a variety of reasons, including the widely held view that every child needs a father or a social equivalent, the financial plight of female headed families, the welfare expenditures to support these families, and the perceived effects on children who have no male role model at home (Stack 1974).

Hypothesis Four: Divorce Subsequent to First Birth

1. Changes in Marriage Rates

There have been major changes in marriage rates over the last thirty years. Those changes are most apparent when one looks at differences between ethnic groups, especially African American and European American. As noted earlier, women are marrying at a later age today than before. In 1947 the national marriage rates for those ages 14 to 24 were almost identical for both groups at about 30 percent. The census for Oklahoma shows that by 1960 changes had begun and the trends have continued. As illustrated in Figure 5, the 1960 census report estimated that 34 percent of European Americans ages 14 to 24 were married as compared to 26 percent of African Americans. By the 1990 census for Oklahoma, the marriage rate had dropped to only 13 percent for African Americans and 27 percent for European Americans. For ages 25 to 44, the corresponding rates were 85 percent to 65 percent and in 1990 were 75 percent and 45 percent (Bureau of the Census: 1960a, 1990b). Two trends are reflected in these data. First, the marriage rate is declining for Oklahomans in general, even among those over age 25. Second, the decline is occurring far more rapidly for African Americans than for all other ethnic groups.

In 1960, 23 percent of all Oklahoma males of European ethnicity were single and this figure had increased only slightly (25 percent) thirty years later in 1990. Only about 15 percent of Oklahoman females were single in 1960 and again that figure increased only slightly, to 17 percent in 1990. However, interesting differences appear when comparing ethnic groups. There were about seven percent more non-European American males and females respectively who were single in 1960. The differences in marital status between groups became more apparent in 1990 because of more precise government reporting. For European American males, about 24 percent were single, but the figure nearly doubled for African Americans to 41 percent. On the average, twice as many African Americans in 1990 were single, as compared with European Americans. To summarize, today over 40 percent of all African American males are single, and 34 percent of all African American females are single (Bureau of the Census: 1960, 1990).

2. Divorce Trends

For those who do marry, the prospects of later becoming a single parent are an increasing concern because of the increase in divorce in Oklahoma and nationwide. A number of authors (e.g. Weitzman 1991) have discussed the reasons for the change in divorce rates. The shift to a no-fault divorce pattern is one factor in the increase in divorce rates as it creates a less burdensome route for uncoupling. There is a controversial legislative movement to restrict no-fault divorce in Oklahoma and elsewhere in an effort to reduce the rise in divorce rates among couples with children. A second factor in the increase in divorce rates is the economic independence of women, in spite of their low wage occupational segregation. In Oklahoma, female earners earn approximately 50 percent of what males earn. The third, and perhaps most important factor, is the modification and relaxation of cultural rules concerning divorce and remarriage, discussed below.

3. Demographic Factors

Some of the trends in divorce are purely a result of demographic factors (Kain 1990). As a result of increased longevity, in today's society we have a proportionably truncated reproductive span, coupled with a longer period of time living alone with a spouse after childbearing. Thus, it is not uncommon to spend a considerable period of time with a spouse, up to 40 years, without childbearing duties. Some increase in divorce is simply a result of living with a spouse, and without children, for a longer period of time.

4. Changing Functions of Marriage

Our cultural perceptions regarding the functions of marriage are changing. There is a general trend toward individuation that corresponds with a new cultural rule of seeking a companionate marriage, rather than one based on a necessary instrumental division of labor. It is not surprising, given this set of circumstances, that there has been a significant increase in divorce rates. In fact, in a recent newspaper article in the Lawton Constitution (February 12, 1996), Senator Benson referred to our present state of marriage as "contractual dating" and wanted to make divorce for those with children more difficult to acquire.

The economic impact of divorce for women has been studied by Arendall (1991). In a study of 60 women, he found that 90 percent were pushed below the poverty line or close to it when they divorced. Most of the women were still single four years later when re-interviewed. They could meet their day-to-day expenses, but had little left over for enjoyment. The downward mobility of women who are divorced versus those who remarry is addressed in the present study.

5. Conclusions

Kessler-Harris (1982) described how, with the transition to a wage economy, family prosperity or poverty became closely tied to what individual family members could command for their skills on an open market instead of what they could produce on the land. The decentralization of work and family life changed the family from what once was a self-contained unit of production, which could produce most of what it needed to sustain itself, to a unit of consumption. Subsequently, members of the domestic group sold their skills as human capital on an open market and, in turn, purchased most of what the family needed to sustain itself. This had a profound effect on the occupational structure of female roles and on the nature of poverty. Subsistence goods were purchased at current market prices which were considerably higher than what those items could be produced for in the family. While income in an agrarian economy was unpredictable, and subject to such external influences as loss of productive laborers and natural environmental changes, it was less susceptible to individual earning power and personal skills.

In preindustrial times, to be poor meant not owning land, or tools, or a trade by which to be an independent, self-employed producer; namely, a farmer or craftsman or merchant (Dudley 1988). Or, less frequently, to be poor meant to earn an amount from one's trade or land which was insufficient to sustain the family. The vast majority of the poor in an agrarian society were the property-less workers who were dependent on outside wages. As is the situation in present times, they bought and sold their human capital for what it could command on the open market. These property-less poor were in the minority, however, when compared with those in self-sustaining trades or agriculture (Dudley 1988). It is this segment of the population, namely, the property-less poor, given the increased reliance on a wage economy, which has grown in numbers. With an increasing emphasis on commercial production and increasing technological sophistication, fewer and fewer are able to compete successfully. And, fewer and fewer workers are needed to fill manual labor positions. Furthermore, in a post-industrial economy the distinction between manual and mental labor is becoming less clear—even the fast food worker must acquire some technical expertise.

Family formation strategies do not occur in isolation, but in response to the broader political and economic conditions. Thus, the female headed family today can be viewed as a response to many factors mentioned earlier such as shifts in wage labor, government assistance, and divorce regulations. Today, in family life, we find more variety, fluidity, and idiosyncrasy in all of the major demographic processes such as geographic mobility, marriage formation, marriage dissolution, childbearing, household decision making, and women's personal and working lives. Invariably, according to Tempermen and Wilson (1993), when people have a greater opportunity to choose—a mate, a living arrangement, the number of children they will bear—they exercise this choice. Traditional constraints begin to fall with the exercise of new choices and the cultural definition of these choices.

These new choices, however, are not free choices as one might at first be inclined to think. They are subject to economic constraints and larger cultural processes such as cultural rules and institutions. These arguments help to explain why the family formation strategies in our post–modern society are so different than those of an agrarian, early industrial, or 1950s society.

Methodological Approaches To Poverty Cycles

1. Previous Research on Poverty Cycles

Bane and Ellwood (1983) reviewed the "Panel Study of Income Dynamics" (PSID) data, a longitudinal study of 4,000 persons in poverty. Length of time in poverty was one factor studied. They found that at any given time about 60 percent of those in poverty will remain there eight or more years. This group is termed Welfare Dependent in the present research. On the other hand, they found that most who become poor at some point in their lives are only poor for one or two years. These are referred to as Temporary Poor in the present study. By the time a person has been poor for three years, according to Bane and Ellwood's analysis, they are far less likely to escape poverty. Specifically they found that 41 percent of those who are beginning a poverty spell will escape within one year, 59 percent within two years, and over two-thirds (69 percent) within three years. Beyond that point, however, only 27 percent of those who have been poor for three years will escape within the next two.

Bane and Ellwood (1983) also found that parental SES was a significant predictor for long-term poverty. They found that 20 percent of poverty spells of children begin at birth. However, at any point in time, a child who becomes poor because of a change in family structure from married to single headed will likely enter a poverty episode lasting almost ten years. Bane and Ellwood further found that the majority of welfare dependent mothers tend to be ethnic minorities, never married and high school drop outs.

In addition to measuring the length of time in poverty, Bane and Ellwood (1983) also examined the causes for entering and exiting poverty. According to their research, fewer than 40 percent of poverty *spells* begin with a change in income earnings. While this was the largest single cause of movement into poverty, it suggests that one cannot understand the bulk of poverty by simply understanding fluctuations in earnings of the family head. Importantly, only 14 percent of poverty episodes for female heads of households begin with a drop in earnings. Rather, their research found that female headed poverty typically began when the female headed family was formed either through separation/divorce or when an unmarried female had a child. Thus, the major reason a female entered poverty was because she became head of a family. The present study also estimates the relationship between female headship, marriage and poverty.

More poverty periods for female heads in the PSID data ended with a change in earnings than began with such. Nearly 34 percent of poverty periods ended as a result of increased earnings by the female head. Moreover, changes in the earnings of "others" classified as living in the household, either an older child or another adult not classified as head, also accounted for an additional 22 percent of the movement out of poverty for female heads. (This could very likely account for the incorporation of a live-in partner.) Marriage was the second most important route out of poverty, accounting for 27 percent of upward mobility. Reasons for movement out of poverty are also addressed in the present study.

In addition to female householders, another segment of society is extremely vulnerable, namely, the lower wage earners or working poor, who may dip into occasional poverty. For example, Coe (1978), in research similar to that of Bane 1994; Bane and Ellwood 1983; and Ellwood 1993 found that only about half of the poor were poor for more than five years. And only about one percent were poor nine out of nine years. Coe (1978), however, found that fully 25 percent (as compared to the overall poverty rate of 14 percent) of Americans were poor at least one year out of the nine, and these were usually working poor who, because of a change in personal circumstances, dipped temporarily into poverty. These families are referred to as Temporary Poor and Cyclers in the present research.

In fact, Coe (1978) estimates the circulation of persons within poverty to be as high as 40 percent. He notes that as much as 40 percent of the American public has been poor, as defined by the official poverty line at some point is their lives. What this means is that while the percent of poverty resulting from structural or economic/political factors consistently remains stable at around 14 percent, the circulation mobility (who is in poverty) is greater, at around 25 to 40 percent. Finally, Coe (1978) found that is not an either/or situation, with approximately half of heads of poor families being employed at least part of the time. These families are referred to as the Combiners in the present research because they combine work with government and kinship aid or as Cyclers who fluctuate between work and welfare. The terms Cyclers and Combiners were originally used by the Institute for Women's Policy Research (IWPR). The Institute found that 23 percent of women on welfare were Cyclers and 20 percent were Combiners (1993).

Conclusions

A biocultural approach to the study of poverty looks at how the economy literally gets under the skin (cf. Thomas 1994; Thomas, Brooke, Winterhalder 1979; and others). The hidden dimension is biology. We have cultural rules (emic view or conditional rationality) that guide behavior or adaptive strategies. However, tensions such as political restructuring lead to biological adaptations and new cultural rules and family formation strategies. We used to think of biology and culture as complementary, but today the question asked by some biocultural anthropologists is whether culture may be impairing biology as a result of increasing system perturbations given increasing global competition, rapidly changing technology and corporate restructuring. The present research assesses the degree to which reproductive and family formation strategies such as early childbearing and female headship may have long-term associated costs and benefits.

NOTES

1. A very different picture exists in 1990 depending upon whether one looks at educational attainment for all persons over the age of 25, or for only those persons between the ages of 24 and 35. If we look all persons age 25 and over, we find that 18.5% of White males have Bachelors' degrees. About 31% of Black males in the same cohort have finished high school, but only 9% or half as many have completed college. For American Indian 27.5% finished high school and 9.5% college. For Hispanic only 20% have finished high school but of those about the same as other groups or 8.5% finished college. More Asian (21%) have college degrees but only 13% have finished high school. The greatest differences occur between the number of White males who have completed college and the Black males and all ethnic minority females, except Asian (General Social and Economic Characteristics, Bureau of the Census:1990).

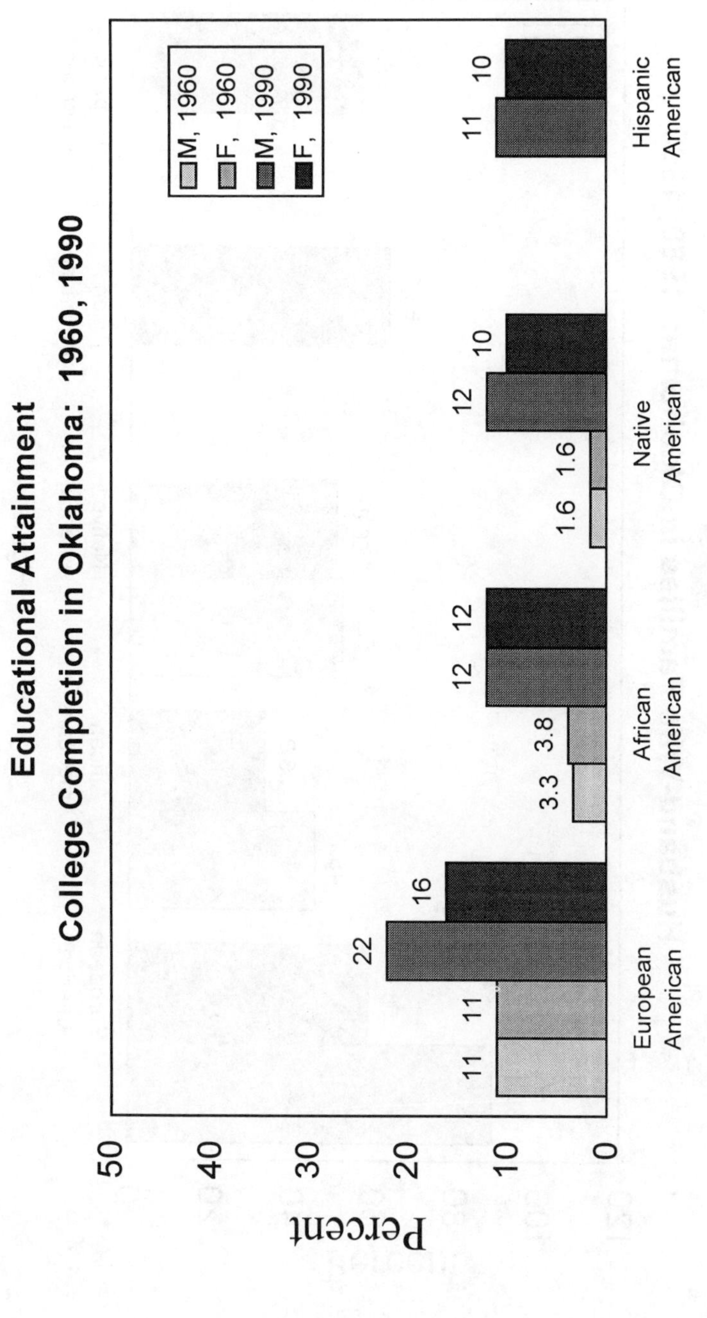

Educational Attainment
College Completion in Oklahoma: 1960, 1990

Legend:
- M, 1960
- F, 1960
- M, 1990
- F, 1990

European American: M 1960 = 11, F 1960 = 11, M 1990 = 22, F 1990 = 16

African American: M 1990 = 12, F 1990 = 12, M 1960 = 3.3, F 1960 = 3.8

Native American: M 1960 = 1.6, F 1960 = 1.6, M 1990 = 12, F 1990 = 10

Hispanic American: M 1990 = 11, F 1990 = 10

Percent (y-axis): 0, 10, 20, 30, 40, 50

Figure 3

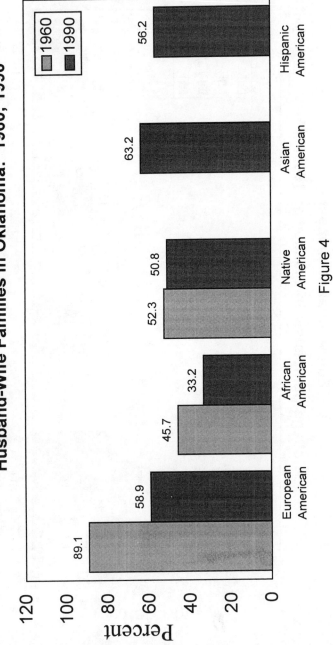

Marital Status
Husband-Wife Families in Oklahoma: 1960, 1990

Figure 4

III
Research Design and Methods

Hypotheses

Stage One: Time Prior to First Birth

Hypothesis One: There is a positive association between parental reliance on government assistance and a female's risk for entering or remaining in poverty at the time of her first birth while adjusting for ethnicity.

Hypothesis Two: Females who experience earlier onset of menarche are more likely to begin sexual intercourse at an earlier age while adjusting for ethnicity.

Hypothesis Three: There is a positive association between the time of first intercourse and age at time of first birth while adjusting for ethnicity.

Stage Two: Time of First Birth

Hypothesis Four: Females who have their first child at a younger age are more likely to enter poverty and do so for more persistent periods than females who have their first child when older, while adjusting for ethnicity and stage one variables.

Hypothesis Five: Females who are unmarried at the time of their first child are more likely to enter poverty and do so for more persistent periods than females who are married at the time of their first child, while adjusting for ethnicity and stage one variables.

Hypothesis Six: There is an interaction between age at first birth and marital status. The proportion of females who have their first child at a younger age and are unmarried at that time are at the greatest risk of entering poverty and do so for the most persistent periods after adjusting for stage one factors.

Hypothesis Seven: There is an interaction between age at first birth, marital status and ethnicity. The rates of age specific parenthood for young, unmarried African American women will be greater than for young, unmarried European American women.

Stage Three: Time After First Birth

Hypothesis Eight: There is an interaction between age at time of first birth and a female's subsequent educational attainment level.

Hypothesis Nine: There is an association between subsequent educational attainment leading to increased earning power and effect on remaining or exiting poverty.

Hypothesis Ten: There is an association between subsequent changes in marital status, either a divorce or a marriage, and a female's risk of entering, remaining in, or exiting poverty.

Hypothesis Eleven: Females who have kinship support as defined as child care, financial or shelter will be more likely to move above the poverty level.

Research Design

1. Introduction

Poverty can be studied using two types of sample designs, a cross-sectional snapshot in time or a longitudinal video through time. Given the importance of understanding the heterogeneous and dynamic makeup of poverty in the U.S. and to most accurately capture the specific cycles of poverty that any one family might experience, this research study used a life cycle rather than cross sectional sample design. Such a design is more likely to assess the degree of mobility versus persistence of poverty over the family life span and the complex reasons a female is likely to dip in and out of poverty. Additionally, the present study expanded on previous poverty research by Bane and Elwood (1983); Furstenburg (1991, 1992); Geronomus (1991); Hogan and Kitawaga

(1985); Lancaster (1986, 1989); Stack (1974); Wilson (1987, 1991) and others in several important ways. Not only was the present research diachronic in design but, specifically, this study examined the potential causes of poverty within a three stage, temporal model that integrated biological, cultural, and societal risk factors.

2. Stage One: Time Prior to First Birth

Stage one estimated the effects of primarily ascribed characteristics over which the female had little control, either because they were inherited or were features of the social structure. The variables of interest in stage one were primarily associated with parental socioeconomic status during the female's teen years. The composite measure of this predictor combined several important variables that were reported in the literature to be surrogate measures of a person's social and economic position (e.g. Hogan and Kitagawa 1983). The composite measure was calculated by ranking each parent's occupation and place of employment, the degree to which the parents relied on government assistance, age at which the females' sisters first gave birth, the type of family of origin structure, and finally, the female's perception of the degree of overcrowding in the home while growing up.

3. Stage Two: Time of First Birth

Stage two in the model focused on certain achieved characteristics that were based on choices the female made regarding sexual activity and intimate partnerships. The variables of interest at this stage were the female's age and martial status at the time of her first birth. Because the term "teen birth" may include those pregnancies at 18 or 19 which generally occur after the female and her partner have completed school, this research follows Lancaster's (1986) important distinction of "school age" pregnancy (17 or younger) rather than lumping all teen pregnancies together. Teen pregnancy was therefore measured as those who gave birth at age 17 and younger compared to age 18 and older. Because of the small sample size, age at first birth was also estimated as a continuous variable. The continuous interval measure of age was used in the multivariate analysis.

The second major risk factor assessed at stage two was the female's marital status at the time of her first child. A woman was considered as "married" if she cohabitated with or was legally married to a partner at the time of the birth or within three months after the birth, and regardless of whether the couple was living on their own or with relatives. Additionally, the couple, whether legally married or not, had to reside together for at least six months before an estimate of the effect of marriage on poverty was evaluated. There are several other variables that were taken into account at this and subsequent stages in the life cycle; namely, the degree to which the couple or female relied on kinship aid, management of child care, the ability to complete an education, and the ability to obtain and maintain steady employment. Each of these variables is discussed in the Ethnographic and Statistical Analysis sections.

While the major predictors of poverty at stage two were the age at which parenthood begins and whether the female was married at that time, the effects of these additional factors cannot be ignored. Indeed, the means by which a female could buffer herself from the most devastating of poverty periods may not necessarily be a spouse but instead rest on the ability to complete an education, delay the onset of a second birth, availability of kinship support, and stable employment during which child care and transportation are manageable. The effects of these mediating factors are evaluated in the Statistical Analysis chapter.

4. Stage Three: Times Subsequent to First Birth

Stage three in the model was the time subsequent to the onset of parenthood. Certain factors at stage three would increase the risk for entering and remaining in poverty while others would reduce that risk, or at least, increase the chances of getting out. The primary question of interest at stage three was whether a divorce or marriage occurred for females who were ever married, whether the marriage occurred by first birth or at some point thereafter. Other variables of interest at this stage were the effects of remaining unmarried, subsequent educational attainment, present occupational ranking, total number of dependents, and the female's access to health care coverage. The major predictors of poverty at this stage were a decrease or increase in earnings because of a divorce or marriage. The effect of never marrying was also compared to being divorced or currently married in instances where the male was employed and the female was a homemaker. The major variables that could mitigate the effects of poverty at this stage were a change to a husband-wife family formation, or in the case of the unmarried female, gaining sufficient, subsequent education and a skilled occupation that resulted in a favorable change in her earning power.

5. Significance of the Temporal Model

Not all the variables will have equally significant effects on the outcome of poverty. For example, in stage one, parental SES was expected to have the greatest effect, while in stage two the most likely predictors for entering poverty were age and marital status at first birth. In stage three the greatest predictors for exiting poverty were likely a change to a husband-wife family and additional educational attainment; whereas the highest risk for entering poverty was a change to a female headed family structure because of divorce. While the individual variables may be important predictors of poverty, this research also assessed whether the cumulative effect of the major risk factors increased the likelihood of a female entering and remaining in poverty. To reiterate, while each of the variables in the model had the potential to increase a female's chance of becoming and staying poor, this model suggests that certain ones are more powerful predictors than others and that these occurred at different points in her life cycle.

What is important about the three-stage, temporal model suggested herein is that it incorporates a life span approach to poverty. The risk for entering poverty can occur at any time in the model, and potentially through any single variable. However, as the effects at each stage become cumulative, the probability is greater that the poverty period will continue. The separate and cumulative effects of each of the four independent variables were tested in a multivariate regression model (see Statistical Analysis section). Frequencies and correlation estimates measured the relationship between each of the minor variables and the degree of poverty for each of the 47 females. The regression model was limited to the four major independent variables due to the small sample size.

A second important feature of the multistaged approach to studying poverty is its ability to distinguish between temporary, cyclical and persistent poverty. For example, a young married couple might have experienced a short dip into poverty when just starting out. On the other hand, an unmarried female might have experienced a temporary poverty spell after giving birth, but only until she completed her interrupted education. This model therefore builds on the important finding by Bane and Ellwood (1983) and others that debunks the myth that the poor are a fairly stable subculture living on the welfare rolls. Indeed, the literature suggests that as many as one-third of the poverty population may shift in or out of poverty in any given year. Such findings are potentially corroborated in the present research and have important implications for welfare reform.

To summarize, the majority of poverty research tends to be cross-sectional and focuses on individual characteristics of the poor or on intervention strategies. In part, this is because of the difficulties in tracking and following a specific sample or cohort of persons over time. However, such cross-sectional snapshots in time do not mirror the complexities of women's lives through time. For this reason, in spite of the difficulties of tracking one group of women, in doing so, the present research was better able to capture the reality of the heterogeneous makeup of those in poverty and the spells or periods of poverty that may occur during a female's life cycle.

Figures 5 and 6 represent the conceptual framework for the research design of this study. The four independent variables that were entered into the regression model are displayed graphically with bold lines.

Sample Design

1. Initial Sample

The first interview with study participants occurred when they were pregnant and visited the Oklahoma Memorial Hospital or either of two Family Medicine Clinics for prenatal care from the fall of 1988 to the fall of 1991. The original study was conducted by the University of Oklahoma Health Sciences Center with Dr. Troy Abell, Principal Investigator. The initial objective of the project was to investigate the etiology of intrauterine growth retardation and prematurity (Abell 1989). A sample of 1,250 women participated in the study funded by the National Institute of Child Development (NICHD RO1 HD20511) with Institutional Review Board approval.

These women were recruited at their initial prenatal visit at the Oklahoma Medical Hospital's (OMH) Women's Clinic or either of two Family Medicine Clinics in Oklahoma City, Oklahoma. Criteria for eligibility included being at least 18 years of age (at this birth) or obtaining parental consent, and verbal competency in English. The criteria for exclusion were multiple gestation, known fetal congenital abnormalities, being under the care of a correctional or mental institution, or receiving psychotropic drugs for the treatment of mental illness. Signed consent to participate in the study was obtained from all women 18 years of age or older or from a parent of women younger than 18. At the initial prenatal visit, a researcher briefly explained the project; each patient was assured that participation was strictly voluntary and decisions about participation would in no way impinge upon her medical care. Initial data collection included: (1) an interview, pelvic exam, and anthropometric assessment at the initial medical prenatal visit and at approximately 32 weeks gestation; (2) a neonatal assessment of the infant between 24 and 36 hours of birth; (3) a postpartum anthropometric assessment of the mother; and (4) chart abstraction of each medical prenatal visit.

At the initial prenatal visit and at the 32 weeks of gestation follow–up interview, participants were engaged in a structured interview. Questions yielded sociodemographic data, medical and contraceptive history, family attitudes towards pregnancy, health behaviors, and child care plans. The major objective of the initial pregnancy study was to estimate the determinants of low birth weight; however, data on important sociodemographic variables and household structure were also collected. These variables included household composition and size, income, female participation in the labor force, previous births, previous pregnancies, parental SES, and health and life style factors.

It is important to note that the original sample was delineated by two critical factors, namely, females who received obstetrical care at the OMH Women's Clinic or two Family Medicine Clinics and who agreed to participate in the study. An important issue which must then be addressed is whether the trends identified in this study are generalizable and reflective of trends among the urban poor population in general. Or, is the portrait captured by the original researchers and subsequently in the present research peculiar to the study sample? Support for the generalizability of the initial findings to other low income populations comes from research by Metcoff's study of maternal nutrition and fetal growth among 2,400 low income women in Oklahoma (1981) and the Oklahoma State Department of Health's Maternal and Child Health Service's 1991-92 statewide pregnancy assessment data (discussed in the Statistical Analysis chapter).

2. Follow Up Sample

The present study is a follow up on a subset of the original study participants. In the summer of 1995, approximately five years after the initial interviews with the women, the first phase of the follow–up study began. It was conducted by students enrolled in a University of Oklahoma ethnographic field school directed by Dr. Troy Abell. The researchers attempted to re–contact as many of the 1,250 patients from the original sample as was possible during the six-week field school. Researchers attempted to contact every initial study participant using the latest telephone numbers listed on their hospital medical records. The four research teams were able to complete follow–up interviews with 70 of the original study participants during the summer field school. At the time the researchers conducted these interviews, each study participant was asked if she would consent to an additional follow–up interview which focused on such women's issues as child and health care, intimate relationships and strategies for supporting a family. It is these second follow–up interviews that form the basis for the research presented herein. Almost without exception (three declined) each female agreed to be re-contacted for the second, more indepth follow–up interview. The second set of interviews were conducted an average of 30 to 120 days following the summer field school.

Of a potential sample of 67 females who originally consented to the additional interview, 47, or 70 percent, actually participated. The other 20 women were unable to be interviewed for a variety of reasons. Some women subsequently declined a second interview when contacted or would not return messages left at the point–of–contact telephone number. Others agreed to the interview but repeatedly failed to be home at the appointed time. The majority, however, simply could not be reached because their telephone numbers had already changed by the time the second interview was attempted. It is, therefore, important to note that those who participated in the second series of interviews do not constitute a random sample. They constitute a convenience sample consisting of those who were able to be contacted by the summer field school researchers and who agreed to be re-interviewed on two separate occasions. The implications of these sample limitations are addressed in the Discussion chapter of the book. It should be noted that an additional 55 persons were reached during a subsequent field school just prior to publication and their life cycles are presently being studied.

Given these circumstances, the subset sample that constitute the second series of interviews is then characterized by having one or more of the following five defining characteristics. It consists of women who may have especially been interested in the research on children's health, or were compliant because they wanted to *help out* or felt they *had to* since they had agreed to participate in the research five years ago. Second, the sample is defined by those who may have recently received medical attention at the Oklahoma Clinics and, therefore, had newly updated telephone numbers on their medical records. A third defining feature is that some women may just happened to have been in the same place as five years ago, either because they were some of the more stable of the original sample or, because of a recent change in life circumstances, were currently living with relatives whose telephone numbers were listed as the point of contact. A fourth defining feature of the sample is that the interviewee may have changed residence, but could still be contacted by the "other," usually a relative's, telephone number found on her medical records. This last characteristic suggests that the sample may be biased toward those who have a geographically close kinship system. A final crucial feature is that the sample consists of those who happened to be home at one of the numerous times the summer field school researchers attempted to contact them and agreed to participate in the follow–up series of interviews. Given these considerations, coupled with the original sample selection parameters discussed earlier, it may be difficult to generalize from this sample to women in poverty in general.

Field Work Methodology

The methodological approach of the present study had a structured, as well as an ethnographic, component. The 47 interviews that are the basis for the research were conducted in the homes of the study participants. A research-based living quarters was established in a centrally located part of Oklahoma City, around 42nd and Penn Ave., for seven months. Each female was then contacted by telephone and asked to voluntarily participate in the second follow–up interview. Whenever a study participant agreed to an interview, the researcher drove to her home. Each interview lasted approximately two hours, the shortest being one and a half hours and the longest over three hours. The area traversed included as far away from Oklahoma Medical Center's Women's Clinic and the two Family Medicine Clinics as Arcadia, Moore, Noble, Chickasha, Harrah, Yukon, Hydro, and Luther, Oklahoma.

Each interview incorporated a multi-methodological approach that combined a qualitative life history interview coupled with a structured questionnaire. During the oral history segment, a life chart was compiled that focused on the woman's life around the time of each pregnancy. This segment of the interview proved to be a period of emotional bonding in most cases as the women talked about issues of relationships, children and financial survival. After conducting the oral history interview, the 112 question questionnaire could be completed fairly quickly because many of the circumstances already had been disclosed. By the conclusion of most interviews, there was an appreciation between the researcher and the study participant of the uniqueness, yet similarities, of experiences, dreams and disappointments that occur during a female's life cycle.

The life graph data collection format provided a detailed context surrounding the significant life events for each woman. The structured questionnaire provided the systematic collection of responses to critical items. The fieldwork approach then combined the oral interview regarding the life histories, an ethnographic approach to observing the female's home and interactions with other family members, and a quantitative assessment using the questionnaire. The mix of both qualitative and quantitative field techniques, enabled the creation of profiles of women in poverty. Each profile is developed in the Ethnographic chapter. These profiles incorporate data from the statistical analysis of the interview and questionnaire. Additionally, the profiles are interspersed with quotes and ethnographic observations that illuminate the deep complexities of these women's lives that the quantitative analysis leaves untold.

Statistical Approach

Data from the oral history interview and the questionnaire were entered in SAS and Lotus databases for statistical manipulation. Analyses of the data were on three levels. For all statistical tests of significance, alpha was set at 0.05. The first level of analysis included important summary statistics for each of the major hypotheses. A contingency table summarizes the relative frequencies for the sociodemographics of the sample and each major independent variable (Table 4). Next, major independent variables were compared in relation to the outcomes of Welfare Dependent, Cycler, Combiner, Temporary Poverty and Self Sufficient. The outcome categories were determined by calculating the combined average time the woman was on government assistance and her current economic well-being. The criteria and associations of the independent variables for each poverty outcome are more explicitly reviewed in the Ethnographic chapter.

The second level of analysis compared the odds ratios or Person's correlation coefficients for each of the major hypotheses in order to determine if an association existed and whether it was statistically significant. The odds ratios, correlation coefficients and p values are reported for each hypothesis.

The third level of analysis was multivariate. The multivariate estimates were based on linear regression. The results section lists the unstandardized and standardized regression coefficients and the explained variance for each of the four, time-specific independent variables. The proposed study followed this multivariate strategy, because as anthropologists Fricke et al. (1993:409) state . . . "it permits an examination of a variable's effect in a temporal sequence so as to illuminate whether early life course experiences have effects that are mediated by intervening variables later in life." Thus, for example, if the variable "parental SES" has a significant effect on a woman's risk for entering poverty, and these effects are reduced by stage two or three variables, we may surmise that the effect is mediated by the characteristics, for example, of becoming a parent at a later age or by marrying.

The dependent variable in the regression model is an interval level continuous variable that was measured four ways. The dependent variable was calculated as: (1) net earned and subsidized income, (2) net earned and subsidized income as a percent of poverty, (3) "usable income," and (4) "usable income" as a percent of poverty. Gross, net, and subsidy income were derived by calculating the family's gross and net employment income, child support payments, and government payments of food stamps, AFDC, disability and housing assistance. "Usable income" measured the women's current financial well–being in relation to the corresponding government poverty level for 1995. To calculate usable income, all incoming cash and subsidies were converted to an after taxes monthly income. Next, the monthly mortgage/rent payment and child care costs were subtracted, thereby yielding a "usable income" figure. Housing was subtracted in the usable income models because this appears to be the largest single advantage/liability for those with limited income. For example, a family of four, living in a mobile home paid for by relatives or in a government housing addition, will fare considerably better than a family with the same income who is paying $400 monthly in rent. Housing was not subtracted in the combined earned and subsidized income models.

The gross, net, subsidized, and usable income amounts were then converted to a proportion above/below the current poverty level for that particular family. In that way each family, no matter how poor or well off, could be compared on a regression line according to their relative percentages above or below poverty. The poverty level was calculated using the current monthly government standards for the appropriate family size. The maximum amount of government subsidy a particular family could receive was calculated to determine how much "better off" a family who is not welfare dependent is in terms of monthly usable income. The results are reported in the Statistical Analysis chapter which follows and in Tables 7 and 8.

Multi-stage Conceptual Framework Independent Variables

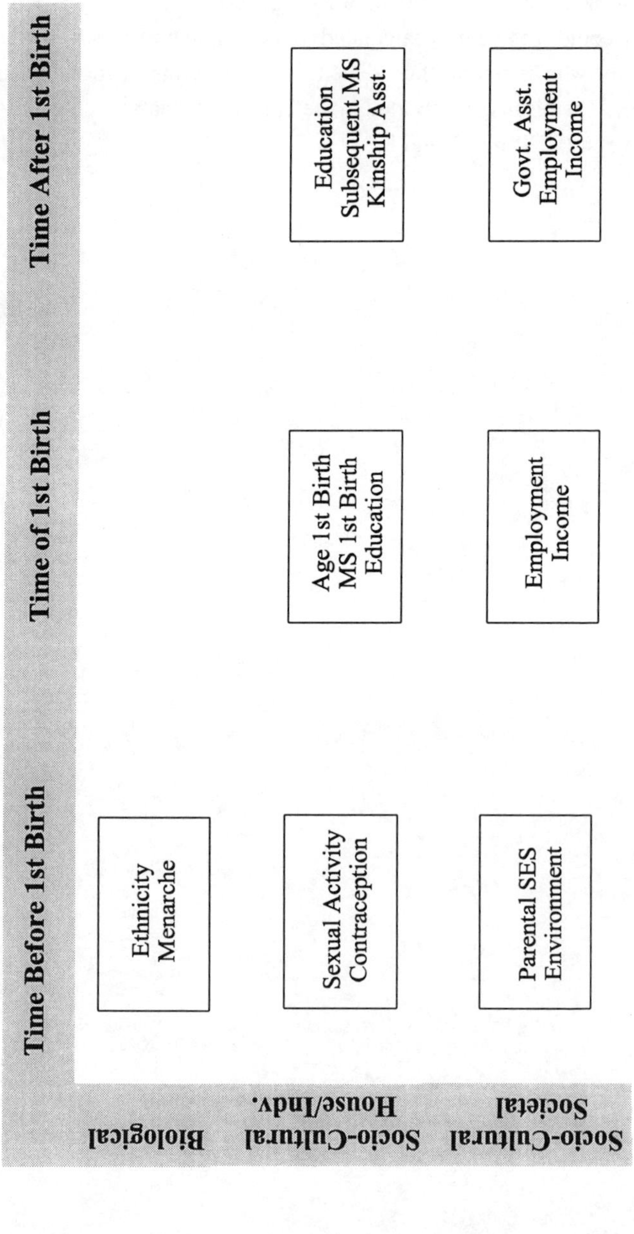

	Time Before 1st Birth	Time of 1st Birth	Time After 1st Birth
Biological	Ethnicity Menarche		
Socio-Cultural House/Indv.	Sexual Activity Contraception	Age 1st Birth MS 1st Birth Education	Education Subsequent MS Kinship Asst.
Socio-Cultural Societal	Parental SES Environment	Employment Income	Govt. Asst. Employment Income

Figure 5

Predictive Model for Risk of Poverty

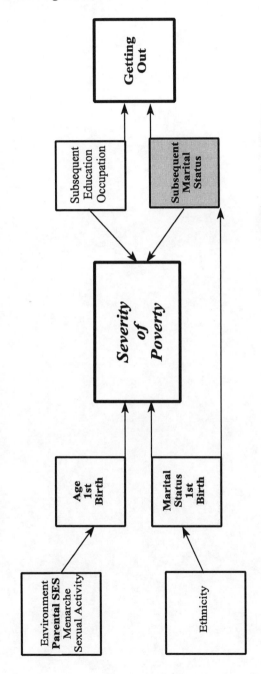

Figure 6

Major Predictors Shaded
Significant Predictor Darkest Shade

IV
Ethnographic Analysis

Introduction

The analysis section incorporates both a qualitative and quantitative approach. The statistical importance of the four major independent variables is discussed in the next chapter. In this chapter, each of the women is classified into one of five general categories or groups of females and a composite sketch of each group's lives is drawn. Group one is composed of females who are "Welfare Dependent," as defined by living totally on welfare for a period of five or more years. Group two represents females who are "Cyclers," as defined by having dipped into poverty for a minimum of two periods during their adult lives, meaning, the period after first giving birth. These poverty periods were usually a result of changes in such life circumstances as job loss, marital status, illness, or pregnancy. Group three consists of females who are "Combiners," most often defined as working poor. They combine either full-time work at low wages or seasonal work at better wages with kinship and/or government aid. Group three does not include those whose sole aid is medical assistance during pregnancies, unless the child remains covered afterwards. Group four is made up of females who are "Temporary Poor," as defined by relying on government assistance for a single period which includes AFDC and/or food stamps, and subsequently have been self sufficient for at least one year. The final group, group five, is those females who have been fully "Self Sufficient," as defined by non-reliance on other than occasional kinship or health care aid. Let us now turn to a discussion of each poverty-type.

Each profile begins with a summary of the major hypotheses and then illustrates the experiences common to women in this poverty category based on one or more case studies from the interviews. Other experiences of women who were interviewed from each category are contrasted with the case studies in order to demonstrate the dynamic and heterogeneous nature of the poverty experience, even within poverty categories. Each profile is based on quotes from the life history oral interviews and item responses to the questionnaire.

Group One: Welfare Dependent

"God made men, so they can't all be bad: but it's hard to find one that's decent."

This profile of the Welfare Dependent female is based on eight cases. For the purposes of this study, welfare dependency is defined as being on full Aid for Families with Dependent Children (AFDC) and food stamp assistance for a minimum of two years and not working during that period. In order to no longer be classified as Welfare Dependent, a female must have been working steadily for a period of at least six months. During that period she must have been able to achieve independent living arrangements as well. Thus, a female who has recently begun working but has been working for less than six months or is still living rent free in her parent's home is also classified as Welfare Dependent. It is therefore possible that some women who are now considered Welfare Dependent have been interviewed midpoint in a temporary poverty cycle or at the beginning of a period of self–reliance and will in the future become Combiners, Cyclers, or Temporary Poor. Which of these women will be able to exit a fully dependent situation, however, cannot be determined at this point. What follows is the story of the Welfare Dependent women I met, as exemplified in the case study of Diane and quotes from interviews with other Welfare Dependent women.

Demographics

In most (5) of the cases these women's parents were also on government assistance. The age at the time they first became parents averaged 18.5 years. The Welfare Dependent women were unmarried at first birth in all but one case. Each woman classified as Welfare dependent is African American. They have never married even though it has been ten years and they are now on the average 28.4 years old. (Or remarried in the case in which the woman was married at first birth but then divorced.) Today, the Welfare Dependent female's net income depends upon the number of persons in the family, but averages $700 per month, all in the form of government subsidies. This includes AFDC and food stamps. In six cases of the eight she also receives fully–subsidized housing in the form of a rent voucher or lives in government maintained housing. This subsidy is valued at approximately $450. These women of poverty and their children also receive full Medicaid medical coverage, but not dental. The following quotes from Diane and other Welfare Dependent women illustrate the life experiences associated with this type of poverty in the United States.

Her name is Diane although it could be Nancy, Sue or Sharon. Today, Diane is 26 years old. She has three children ages three, six and seven. Each child is from the same partner, Chevaz, whom she has been with for seven years. They have never married and lived together only briefly. Diane has been on AFDC and food stamps since the birth of her first child at age 20. She also receives subsidized housing for which her co-payment is $19. Diane is not working, but received some educational training at a business college and job training through various AFDC programs. She was recently given an injection as a form of birth control and has gained 75 pounds as a result of the procedure she was encouraged to try by a physician at Oklahoma Memorial Hospital. Here is her story along with highlights from the stories of other Welfare Dependent women I interviewed.

Growing Up With My Family

For the most part (7 cases), the Welfare Dependent's teen years were spent in a female headed home. Her mom likely worked as a cashier, cook, or in the laundry service sector. In some cases the mother was a homemaker. While growing, up the woman who is dependent on welfare was most likely to live with only a mother, although her mother had important male and kinship relationships. The Welfare Dependent's mother frequently received government assistance, although in some (3) cases, including Diane's, she did not. The female kinship bond was very strong and served as a source of mutual aid and obligation in Diane's case and others who were welfare dependent. Diane stated:

"My mother never received assistance and was extremely strict. I was not allowed out after dark and I was the only girl. She would have shot me if she knew I had sex, so I waited till I was on my own. I've been pretty much on my own since 17, but in the early time I lived with Auntie. I was also close to my to grandma, from who I could *hobo* . . . she just died. Grandma was a midwife and taught me about how to raise a baby."

Bernise, another Welfare Dependent woman, was also raised in a female headed household. She stated:

"My mom has worked most of her life and when I was pregnant she was working two jobs as a shirt presser in two different laundries. My father was killed in his 20s in a double murder in a bar in California."

The women who consistently relied on welfare lived in rural areas such as Okmulgee during their teen years or urban areas such as the Shackleford Commons, a government housing addition, in central Oklahoma City. About one-half the time these women reported the living conditions as crowded to overcrowded while growing up, while the other half of the time they rated them as comfortable. There was an average of 3.4 kids in the family of origin. The sisters of the Welfare Dependent women generally had their first child quite young, on the average at age 17.5. The youngest sister had hers at 13 and the oldest at 21. Around one-third of the sisters of the Welfare Dependent women are on government assistance, while the others are employed in health–related fields such as nurse's aide and retail services such as cosmetology.

Sexual Activity

The Welfare Dependent women reported reaching the age of fertility at around 12 years old or in the seventh grade, as near as they could remember. Many said their parents did not really prepare them for what to expect. On average the Welfare Dependent female did not have sexual intercourse until three or more years after the onset of her menstrual cycle. The average age at which these women first became pregnant was 16. About one-half the time, it was by the first person with whom they engaged in sexual activity. It did not take long for the females in the Welfare Dependent category to get pregnant once they became sexually active; indeed, this is a defining feature for the women in this group. Pregnancy occurred after only about six months for five of the eight women. The interviewees consistently reported that sexual activity most frequently occurred at their parents' or boyfriends' parents' houses, or about half the time at the boyfriend's own home.

Mostly, the women did not use contraception, at least not on a regular basis, primarily because they "did not really think about it." It is not that these women wanted to become pregnant but, as Furstenburg (1992) suggests, it is just that they did not sufficiently not want to become pregnant. The Welfare Dependent women also conceived sooner than the other groups of women, although they did not necessarily initiate sexually activity sooner. Some of the reasons Diane and others reported related to their sexual activity and contraceptive use were:

(Diane) "Just lucky I guess."
(others) "Never really thought about it."
"I did not really know what it was or much about it although I had heard of the pill."
"I actually tried it for a couple of days but it gave me a headache. And anyhow, he said he would pull it out, but he didn't."

The reported time for the second pregnancy varied from five years to only one year. The women who today remain on welfare had their next child on average two-and-one-half years after the first birth. In around one-third of the cases, it was only one year later. Diane's story continued:

"I did not begin having sex until I was living on my own after high school. At first it was with more than one guy. I got pregnant after a few months, but had a miscarriage. After that it took two years to get pregnant again; I was 20 by then."

Others were not so fortunate—as in Glenda's case:

"My first time to get pregnant was at 16. He was the first man I screwed. We did it once or twice a month. I got pregnant right away. Drugs and alcohol were never or rarely involved. I really did not want to get pregnant, but was not using contraception at the time."

My Relationships

Although never legally married, about half of the Welfare Dependent women lived with a partner at some point during the last ten years. The duration of the partnership (all relationships combined) averaged two years. Even when not living together, many had a long–term steady relationship with the partner of their first child, averaging 3.5 years; so, they have not been alone. The partners' ages varied. On average he was only one year older. In two cases, however, the partners were a year younger, and in two others he was considerably older, seven years. Three partners of Welfare Dependent women worked in manual labor positions at the time of the first birth. Others were unemployed or still in school and, therefore, could not support a family. In Diane's case, for example, she has been with one partner since shortly after becoming sexually active and miscarrying during that first pregnancy. She stated:

"At the time (present) me and Greg have been together since I was 19 and have never really lived together except for a few months. The rest of the seven years together we had three kids but lived apart. When we lived together we argued and I didn't like having to cook for him. When by myself, me and the kids could *hobo,* (meaning if she was at her grandma's house she could eat there and so could the kids or she could get a free meal elsewhere). But for him, I would have to cook."

Wayna's experience with men differed. She said:

"I have never been married although I would like to (be) with my last four kids' dad, but he would never make the commitment." Wayna feels she sort of wasted those years of her life since the father of her children ended up marrying someone else on the rebound a year and a half later.

Michelle also would like to marry—her view is:

"God made men, so they can't all be bad: but it's hard to find one that's decent. I think about these things at night and how women tend to talk through stuff and men just do something to take their mind off it. I have been alone since I left Roger a few years ago and it's fine with me. Most men, at least young ones, want to live off your stamps and housing and don't care much about you. If I can find a decent man, then I'll marry."

Education and Employment
Most (5) of the women were in high school when first becoming pregnant. The Welfare Dependent women most commonly were juniors in high school when they first became pregnant; the earliest reported had an abortion in the sixth grade. Diane was an exception as noted earlier. She attributed her late initiation of sexual activity to her strict upbringing. A more common experience is illustrated by Bernise:

"Fortunately, since I was almost finished, I was able to graduate with the assistance of a special school."

It was fairly common for the women in the study, regardless of the poverty category, to become pregnant in their junior or senior year and thus be able to graduate before the actual delivery or shortly thereafter. Among the Welfare Dependent women, 20 percent graduated between the time of conception and having the baby. In three cases the women dropped out upon conception, but all three eventually received a GED or diploma. Again, our case study, Diane was an exception in that she had graduated prior to becoming pregnant, but for most, Welfare Dependent women had to juggle pregnancy and school. Innovative school programs such as the one mentioned above by Bernise were important reasons many were able to complete high school. She stated:

> "I had to drop out with my first child because I was sick and couldn't handle the classes. I had to have bed rest. But I got pregnant again the next year and went back and was able to finish with my second child because the school opened a nursery and the girls could come to school with their kids and leave them in the nursery while they attended class. We all took turns as the baby sitters during different periods. I gave a lot of advice because I was the only one who already had a kid."

Often AFDC remuneration requires that a woman return to school or seek employment. The high school diploma is the first step and can be a major hurdle once having dropped out of regular high school. Marie, another of the Welfare Dependent women illustrates this point:

> "Getting my GED was really hard—had to write essays." Marie said, her kids will stay in school and finish and not drop out like she did. "I failed it (GED) twice and welfare only pays to take it twice but I passed the final section on the third try my family paid for that one." Marie is now going to Vo-Tech.

Government subsidized child care enables women such as Marie to attend Vo-Tech or other educational facilities and she is looking forward to working full–time, but is worried. She exemplifies a concern that many of the women expressed about child care, especially once it is no longer covered by government assistance. Marie stated:

> "I will have to make other arrangements for child care at that point—couldn't afford to pay." Her mom lives close but is too tired when she gets home from cleaning houses and Marie

doesn't want to ask her for help. "Mom flips on the TV," she said, "and sits on the couch with the remote; her feet sore from cleaning."

Diane, our featured case, echoing Marie's concerns regarding child care, stated:

"I was working two jobs when I had my first child and I traded off child care with a friend in order to work. She is concerned about day care now that she is trying to go back to work because, "Some daycare don't open on weekends or evenings when people work late. Many of the jobs for me and others without a college education are not nine–to–five but daycare usually operates like that."

Another common problem for many of the Welfare Dependent women and others I interviewed was their inability to work because of health problems, either theirs or their child's, either during or after pregnancy. The doctor often ordered bed rest during the pregnancy, or the nature of the job made it difficult for a woman to continue working. In three Welfare Dependent cases, the woman was working the first time she conceived. In Susan's case the heavy lifting was no longer feasible after pregnancy:

"Because I could not lift the patients (after pregnancy) as a nurse's aide at the hospital, they fired me."

A final work-related problem many of the women face was reliable transportation as clearly evidenced by Diane, the featured case study's current situation:

"I've mostly been a cook and am not working now but have from time–to–time had jobs for a few months and during that time been off assistance or on reduced benefits. I don't much want to go back to school and would like to get on my feet and get a job."

She went on to say:

> "I bought a car and made two payments on time and just threw
> away the money, because it's broken and the dealer won't fix it
> except to add the cost of the repair to my payment. So it's just
> sitting in the driveway till they come and get it. I've had it only
> two months and he won't help so he'll come and get the car back
> next week. He (dealer) feeds off of people. He came in the
> middle of the night with a wrecker and picked up the car last
> month and I had to prove I had made the payment before they
> would let the car down. No warning—they just jacked up the car
> at three in the morning. I heard it and ran out and had to search
> for that month's pay receipt at that moment or the car would
> have been towed and now it's broken so he still gets it back and
> I made every payment right on time."

Government and Kinship Assistance

Every Welfare Dependent woman expressed desires similar to Diane's;
that is, to begin working and be self-sufficient if they could overcome the
tremendous roadblocks of child care, transportation, and manage
financially once the supplemental assistance they receive is reduced or
withdrawn. Bernise reflects the desires and concerns associated with
working. Bernise just got her first job after being on assistance since she
got pregnant as a senior in high school. She had been on assistance for
seven years. Although still living with her mother, she has been working
for six months as a housekeeper at an upscale retirement home:

> "The ladies always call for me and one other one when they need
> something and they talk about finding us a man. They give us
> tips when we do things for them."

Bernise's eyes lighted up as she mused about whether the nursing
home residents would give her tips at the holidays as they do now when
she does things for them. One of the few women in the study to receive
health benefits from their employers, Bernise will begin to receive full
health benefits, including dental, after one year. She is off AFDC for the

first time since getting pregnant in high school. Bernise earns $5.00 an hour. The sad irony is that her $300 in monthly food stamps will now be reduced considerably because of the $800 per month she earns. Bernise and her three children are living with her mother because they can not afford to live separately on her salary. Bernise is waiting to get on Section 8 and views this as a way to become independent and live away from home. Sixty dollars (30%) of her $200 weekly paycheck is deducted for taxes (not deducted when on government assistance) and health benefits (received at no cost under Medicaid), so she lives on $640 a month. But, she said:

"It's the gross they go by for welfare, not what you get."

Bernise demonstrated the plight of many women who wish to become self-reliant. As a productive worker in our society, Bernise is working for the equivalent of $0.17 an hour (or a net income of $30 more per month) more than she could receive on government assistance. Government assistance appropriations would also include medical coverage. Bernise's net benefit of $0.17 per hour does not take into account clothing, food, transportation costs, or child care complexities when she is no longer living with her mother. The net 17¢ per hour likewise does not consider the nonmaterial benefits (informal utilities) of being *off welfare*, feeling needed and appreciated by the ladies at the *home,* being out of the house and making new friends, and her new feeling—apparent in her smile—of being *almost* independent.

While Bernise in the above scenario lived with relatives, others lived in Section 8 or Housing Urban Development (HUD) government-assisted housing. There is an average wait of three years in order to receive such assistance. Wayna, another Welfare Dependent woman whom I interviewed, managed to find satisfactory Section 8 rental property after waiting for two years to become eligible:

"I've lived in this house for five years. The children's father fixes it up or I should say maintains it. I waited two years to get on housing. It's when you first apply, you need it".

Wayna pays $16 of the rent which is $475 (per month). The rest is covered by a (Section 8) voucher to the landlord. Wayna went on to say, "It took awhile to find a decent house in a good place for the kids." The kids do not go anywhere for day care. The older kids help her with child care. When I was in her home supper was cooking and one child went to pick up another from school because . . . "it was time to do so."

Some women living in HUD housing complexes were not so fortunate. Diane's experiences in HUD housing reflected the concerns for the safety of their children that so many women expressed. When I interviewed Diane she had been in her present place for six months after living in her previous HUD housing for four years. When I arrived Diane was just finishing breakfast and was waiting for me. Another female relative was there watching TV. A while later a senior citizen's bus came by, beeped the horn, and dropped off a two-week-old baby. It was her cousin's child. Diane's mother was originally watching the infant, but was going to a senior citizen's activity. So the driver of the bus dropped off the baby to Diane to watch for a couple of hours. As we subsequently continued the interview, Diane talked of life in federally funded housing complexes. As will be seen below, Diane's HUD housing experience reminds us of the dangers of the central city neighborhoods. She stated:

> The first HUD housing she and her kids lived in for four years was at the Bar S Court complex. She stated, "Had one person shot in the front of the house and one person shot in the back yard." At that point Diane found a Section 8 rental and moved for her kids' sake, ". . . because I don't want them to grow up seeing things like that."

Section 8 also has associated problems. It appears that landlords escalate rental fees in housing which is federally subsidized. A conservative estimate, based on the present study, projects that the housing is at least $75 overpriced in a typical HUD or Section 8 subsidized home. Some of the women, such as Susan, another Welfare Dependent woman who lives in government housing, seemed to occupy homes that were devoid of personal attachments and reminded one of the barren and transient cement prisons which encapsulate many modern urban dwellers. Susan's housing seemed to reflect little of her personality:

> When I arrived Susan picked up a few things like coats and stuff; otherwise, the place was clean and had just been vacuumed. Her five kids and an adult male cousin were there. He lives with them and provides a male role model for the kids. What I noticed was that the house didn't have much in it. The living room contained only two couches and a TV on a low table. There were two sets of pictures on the wall and one pair of curtains split between two windows. Susan said that the neighbors speak from time to time, but after living there for two years and two months, the neighbors don't visit or exchange errands with each other. She said, "We all keep pretty much to ourselves."

Housing assistance can make the difference in whether a woman can make it or not. Diane stated:

> "I receive a $490 voucher which covers the total rent payment, $509 in AFDC, and $428 in stamps, plus full medical."

Unfortunately, when a woman's personal or financial circumstances change there is a time lag in concurrent benefit changes. In the allotment illustration above, Diane, our case study, reported that she was taken off assistance for one year because her case worker came to visit while Diane was staying with her cousin. Her cousin said Diane was not living there for fear of losing her own disability coverage. As a result, Diane lost her benefits, she said, and it took a year to be reinstated. During the year Diane was taken off assistance, she made sure the kids were taken care of. She said:

> "I sent two kids to live with their father's mother; I had to."

If paternity has been established or child support awarded by the courts, the Department of Human Services (DHS) will attempt to enforce its payment. Yet the woman does not actually benefit from this endeavor. For example, AFDC contacted Susan's partner for child support. When they located Kevin, Susan received $50 of the $200 they took out of his paycheck. The government kept the rest to makeup for the AFDC she received when Kevin should have been paying child support. Even had DHS given her the full amount, it simply would have proportionately been deducted from her current AFDC entitlement. When Susan and Kevin, her partner, found out what was happening and that they ". . . were losing $150 to the government . . . he just quit his job."

Dreams for the Future

Diane stated: "The major issues I have to contend with is the safety of my children and their success in life."

Bernise reflected: "I'd like to get the kids into a house and get dependable transportation."

Wayna mentioned: "I can pay the bills but there isn't a lot left over. I worry if the money is going to be there when the kids need shoes."

Susan mused: "Now that the kids are older, what am I going to do with the rest of my life."

Finally, Marie reflectively stated: "As for men, if there aren't any decent ones around, I would rather be alone."

Some of the life themes the women mentioned were: "Don't Worry. Be Happy" and "The Old Woman in the Shoe."

Group Two: Cyclers

"We had planned to marry but the baby came first. "

To be classified as a Cycler a woman must have experienced a minimum of two distinct periods of poverty lasting at least six months per period. The Cycler is further defined by having a period between cycles in which they were off AFDC for a minimum of six months. During these six months, the Cycler needed to be self-reliant or receiving only food stamps. It is quite possible that a Cycler will, over time, become a Combiner or self–reliant depending upon her life circumstances. This profile of the Cycler is based on eight interviews.

Five women who are classified as Cyclers are currently employed. One of the male partners is employed. The women average $750 take-home pay per month at their jobs while the single, employed male partner nets around $1,500 per month. In addition to employment income, Cyclers receive between $225 to $800 per month in government subsidies. Housing is paid for by government assistance in two cases and by parents in another.

Demographics

In three of eight cases, the Cyclers' parents were also on government assistance. The average age at the time a Cycler first became a parent was 20.5, which is two years older than the Welfare Dependent group. One-third of the women in this group were unmarried (including one who was married but separated) at the time of their first birth and two–thirds were married. In contrast to the Welfare Dependent group, Cyclers are mostly European American. Specifically, they are European American in six cases, Native American in one, and African American in the other. Cyclers have an average of three children. It is important to note that half of those who were married at the first birth subsequently divorced, and, consequently, experienced a downward spiral into poverty. In only one case (African American) has a woman who cycled in and out of poverty never married. Six of the Cyclers are currently single, separated or divorced. Thus, while the majority of the women in the Welfare

Dependent and Cycler groups are currently unmarried, the routes to female headship differ, thus corroborating the trend noted by other researchers. They found that there are different routes to female headship between African American and European American women; these are never marrying versus divorce.

In the present study most Cyclers were European American and they followed the trends found in previous research; specifically, they cycled into poverty because of a change in family structure due to divorce or job loss, rather than never marrying. Their reasons for exiting poverty were a change in earnings because of beginning, returning or changing jobs in four-fifths of the cases and marriage in one-fifth of the cases. Cyclers are an average of 30 years old today. It has been around nine years since they first gave birth. Five of the employed Cyclers net an average net income between $500 and $900 per month. The one employed male partner earns two to three times more than the females. Over half of Cyclers currently subsidize their employment income with stamps, disability, or housing. The greatest number of poverty cycles experienced by the women is five, while the average number is two. The average period of time for a cycle of poverty is quite varied and ranges from less than six months to over eight years depending on the person and the type of subsidy she received. What follows is the story of the women I met who cycle in and out of poverty as exemplified in the quotes from the case study of Nancy and the other Cyclers who were interviewed.

The quotes from these interviews illustrate the life experiences associated with this type of poverty in the United States. I chose to highlight Nancy's experiences because she represents those who enter poverty because of health reasons, and they are an often forgotten segment of the poor community. I will also illustrate the cases of Marcie and Terry who cycle in and out of poverty because of marriage and divorce. First, let us turn to the case of Nancy.

Today, Nancy is 26 years old. She has three children; their ages are five, six and seven. Each child is from her partner, Brandon, whom she has been with for six years. They were married three months after their first child was born and are still married. Nancy had a miscarriage at 15 after she ran away from home and was raped. She had her first live birth at age 20. Nancy and Brandon have been receiving AFDC for two years, as a result of a work–related disability and her need to care for him. They have received food stamps periodically, depending upon his ability to work. Brandon has been on disability off and on for four years because of an injury to his knees and several required surgeries. Nancy's life is highlighted in the illustrations below, along with Marcie, Terry, and others.

Growing Up With my Family
In slightly less than two-thirds of the cases a Cycler's teen years were spent in a female headed home. The family of origin received government assistance in two of the cases. Often the women's fathers worked in upper level manual positions such as oil, steel and automotive. Their mothers were most often homemakers but if employed, it was in the social and health care services. Nancy, who was introduced in the case study, mentioned:

> "My mother was a homemaker and my father received social security because he was legally blind. This was the only type of government assistance we ever had. I don't see my parents as much as I do my brothers and their families. But I do see my mom sometimes when I help her out at the snack bar they have— when her diabetes is acting up."

Marie, also a Cycler, who currently lives in HUD housing and has been divorced for eight years had this to say about growing up:

> "My mother was on government assistance for quite some time until her marriage to my stepfather when I was a teen. Before that my real father was abusive." Marie reported remembering that as a child he was mean to her and her sisters. She can only remember bits and pieces such as being asleep and then waking up in a different house, realizing that at some point during the night her mother had moved them. She said, "I was scared not knowing the bedroom and then as it grew lighter I realized I was in my aunt's (home) and was relieved to be able to recognize the bedroom and ran to the living room where I saw familiar faces."

Marie seemed to think that the nightly evacuations to her aunt's occurred more than one time.

In Terry's case growing up was fairly pleasant. As an adult, however, her relationship with her family changed dramatically. Terry stated:

"My father disowned me because of my *mixed* child." Terry reported that she grew up in a $100,000 home, but today lives in a HUD housing addition. Her father earns $225,000 a year but ". . . has not even set up a trust for his grandchild or helped me through college because I am still with the father of my child." Terry and Ronaldo have been together for seven years, but they do not live together. She went on government assistance to go to school. Her parents divorced after 20 years and her mother does not know how to earn a living she said, "So, I want to make sure that I can always take care of myself."

Among Cyclers there was an average of 3.3 children in the home while growing up. Only two in this group rated their housing while growing up as crowded; the others perceived theirs as comfortable or spacious. The Cyclers' sisters had their first pregnancy one–and–a–half years younger than sisters of the other women in the study. The Cyclers' sisters gave birth to their first child around 17 years of age on average. The youngest were 14 and 16 years old. Their sisters are currently employed in assembly type work or are homemakers.

Sexual Activity
Around half of the women who cycle in and out of poverty regularly used contraception after becoming sexually active. The most common method of contraception was the pill. As Marie mentioned:

"I got on the pill because I saw my sister and cousin both get pregnant, as did my mother and cousin's mother, as well. I did not want to follow in their footsteps."

Nancy, whose case was illustrated at the beginning of this section, however, did not use contraception. She did not think she could get pregnant because:

> "The rape tore me up so bad." Nancy ran away from home for six weeks because of a fight with her parents when she was a freshman in high school. She was raped by her *pimp* boyfriend while away from home. She was a virgin. After Nancy miscarried, she went home. All subsequent sexual activity has been with her husband, Brandon. "We did it when we first met in a room by the swimming pool at the apartment complex where he did lawn work. His parents owned the complex. Brandon was a virgin. I got pregnant and we married after the baby was born. We're still together."

Four of the Cyclers used contraception. For them, the time between first engaging in sexual activity and the first birth was over three years. Two of the women used birth control pills which they acquired from their parents. Another used a combination of birth control pills and condoms; she acquired the pills from the doctor and the condoms from her partner. The final contraceptive user also relied on condoms. Both women who used condoms stated that their partners purchased them from the store. Almost without exception Cyclers, regardless of their contraceptive practice, began sexual activity at age 16. The frequency of sexual relations for the non-contraceptive–using Cyclers ranged from once a year to twice a month. For the contraceptive users, the range of frequency of coitus was comparable. Cyclers, regardless of whether using contraception, primarily engaged in sexual intercourse at their parent's or someone else's house. For those Cyclers using contraception, the average age of first conception was 20.5 years. Surprisingly, for those not using contraception, the average age was 21.6. (The mean is skewed higher because one women did not conceive until 26.) The non-contraceptive users were just plain lucky for the most part. On average it took more than three years after becoming sexually active before their first child. On the other hand, the majority of the Welfare Dependent who did not practice contraception conceived within six months, even though the frequency of intercourse for both groups is roughly the same.

Intimate Relationships

As stated earlier all of the women who cycled in and out of poverty except two were married when they had their first child, although one was separated. The women were married to partners who were on the average 3.8 years older; whereas the Welfare Dependent women's partners were considerably younger. Two Cyclers had partners nine years older; both of whom had stable employment. Cyclers who were married at the time of their first birth remained married to that partner for an average of four years. However, early marriage is not necessarily an advantage; only two Cyclers are still married to the father of their first child. Their names are Rosa and Karen. During the interview, Rosa stated:

> "We had planned to marry but the baby came first. So we got married one day after the baby was born, right there in the hospital." Rosa and her husband have been married for 11 years. They met when she was 16 and they moved here together from Louisiana.

Karen, who is also still married, did not really think about birth control even though she was living with her husband. They were both young and still in high school. She now has three kids, all of whom have the same father. Karen and her husband, Mike, had to pay cash for the first two children's births but were able to receive medical coverage for the third. They paid off the hospital bill for the first children by making payments—a little at a time. During the interview Karen reflected:

> "We were caught in the middle of not enough money to really cover the birth expenses but too much to qualify for government coverage. I got pregnant six months after I got married and was still in school. We were both working and going to school. His parents would have gotten me the pill but I didn't really think about it. We lived with Mike's parents for two months after we

married." They married after knowing each other only six months. His parents had decided to move and they did not feel right about getting an apartment without being married. " . . .because of our religious views." She was still a senior in high school at the time. Karen stated, "I had the baby one month after graduation. I was 19 years old. We've now been married for seven years."

Not all the Cyclers have been so fortunate in their intimate relationships. Marcie, who was introduced earlier through her nightly evacuations to escape an abusive father, is an example of those less fortunate in mate selection. During her interview she related:

He was proud that he had learned to abuse in ways that the bruises didn't show. Hank learned some of the techniques from his father who was a police officer and who had once held a gun to his wife's head and pulled the unloaded gun's trigger, then laughed. As soon as they married Marcie mentioned she could not even look at another man but he blatantly flirted and received calls at home. Even though it has been eight years since their divorce, Hank still harasses her from time–to–time when he is in between relationships. Today, Marcie lives alone and has regained her self esteem.

Education and Employment
Three Cyclers quit school around three years prior to the birth of their first child. Two women had completed the 10th and one the 8th grade. Contrary to previous reported trends showing lower high school completion rates, each of these women not only eventually completed high school, but acquired additional advanced training at Vo–Tech or college. The other Cyclers had already completed high school by the time of their first child (in one case she completed one month before the delivery). Over half of these women also received training beyond the high school level. In all cases, however, the advanced training is not reflected in their earned income. One reason for the lack of accrued income is because no Cycler or other woman from the study, at the

present time, has achieved beyond an Associate's degree. Thus, most are still largely segregated in low wage service sector occupations. In many cases, high school and/or advanced training was initiated because of AFDC requirements. The minimal effect of advanced training on reducing poverty for women is further addressed in the Discussion Chapter.

Bev is one of only two women in the study who is continuing beyond an Associate's degree. Her efforts demonstrate that a woman's education at the time of first birth does not necessarily predict future educational attainment. Bev is currently divorced and had this to say in regard to her educational goals:

"The first time I got pregnant I was 18 but had been out of school since the 8th grade. So I had been out of school for about three years. I was on general relief when I first dropped out." By the time of Bev's first birth she had completed her GED. She has now finished an Associate's degree and will complete her junior year this year. Bev wants to continue to achieve a Master's degree in psychology. She is currently working at Video Rentals, attending school, and lives cooperatively with her sister, mother, and a roommate since her separation from her husband. Each pays a portion of the house bills.

The complex relationship between working in the service sector for low wages versus reliance on government assistance is reflected in Marcie's situation, the woman introduced earlier who experienced intergenerational abuse from her father and husband. She explained:

"I dropped out of school during the 10th grade but went back after having two children when I was 18 and 19. It was government supported day care assistance, AFDC support, and AFDC requirements that enabled me to get my GED." Marcie, hopes to go back in about a year to become an LPN. She is presently struggling to be self-reliant. Marcie currently works at Briarhouse grocery and has already gotten a raise after being there only eight months. The bad news is that she is up for her second 25¢ raise. This raise will require her to pay a higher

co-payment for her federally supported child care. The net effect
is that her raise will actually mean a decrease in take–home pay,
because of the greater co-payment for child care. The outlook
becomes more dismal for Marcie in the future. When she begins
to earn $6.00 an hour she will lose all medical coverage. She is
now at $5.00 (soon $5.25). Moreover, Marcie cannot receive
health insurance through Homeland grocery unless she is in a
management position; even then, she could not afford the
dependent coverage.

Government and Kinship Support

The length of the poverty cycle and total length of time in poverty varies
from woman to woman. For example, the average length of time Cyclers
have been on food stamps was 16 percent of their adult lives, which is
about one-half of the time of Welfare Dependent women. The longest
period of time that a Cycler received food stamps was 25 percent, and the
shortest was 2 percent of their adult lives. The average length of time
Cyclers were on AFDC also varied. It averaged 11 percent or 3.5 months
of their adult lives. The longest period was 22 percent and the shortest
was 7 percent of their adult lives.

The primary reasons that a Cycler began a period on government
assistance were job loss because of health or injury, as in Nancy's case,
and a change in family structure because of a separation or divorce, as in
Marcie's case. For Rosa also, reliance on government assistance began
with a separation from her husband. A thin, timid woman, who had just
left her husband and traveled 3,000 miles to make a new start at her
mother's home, Rosa related this story:

"When my first child was born I had a good job as a teaching
assistant for retarded adults." Rosa stated that she had medical
coverage for the delivery and was able to take a six month leave
of absence. By the time of her second child two years later,
however, things were different. "I was living with my father
because Timothy and me had separated. I got AFDC, stamps and
Medicaid by signing a statement that my husband was not living
with me and I had no contact with him." By this time Rosa had

completed her GED, by saving to do so when working. She paid a neighbor to watch her child while she worked on her GED. Currently, AFDC is requiring her to return to school full-time. In this situation, the government pays for day care, provides transportation and requires her to apply for a Pell grant to cover tuition. Rosa is attending Vo-Tech where she is studying to be a dental assistant. Her husband stayed in West Virginia to become a musician.

Returning to Nancy and her husband, the case study illustrated at the beginning of this section, their reliance on government assistance was the result of his injury on the job. During the interview, Nancy and Chad painfully recapitulated the following events:

They talked about his surgeries as the primary focus of their life. He can't work for long periods and will need to find a sedentary career because of an injury to his knee while at work. When I asked how they managed, Chad said, "Humor and not letting my troubles overwhelm me keeps me sane." Nancy responded, "Keeping things in perspective works most of the time but then I have to hear from the bill collectors and that gets me down." Nancy reads to reduce her stress.

Nancy continued the story as Chad sat in a chair and listened intently. They are now getting AFDC. However, because the paperwork showing that Chad received $400 a month in disability income was lost, the $470 they received in AFDC included an overpayment for two years. "Now," she stated, "the government is making us pay back $6000 of the AFDC money to makeup for the disability income that wasn't counted." They are entitled to AFDC as long as the wife can show that she has to stay at home to care for her husband. However, because of the overpayment, their AFDC entitlement has dropped from $470 to $40. As a result, Nancy, Chad, and their three children live on $400 disability, $40 AFDC, and $440 food stamps. They meet the eligibility requirements for Section 8 housing but, as noted in other illustrations, it can take an average of three years to begin receiving housing.

Her story continued, "We did okay with the full AFDC but now have to decide which bills to pay and which to leave go." Nancy knows that if she and Chad separated she could get AFDC without it being deducted against his disability. At that moment Chad chimed in, "We're not liars or cheats." Nancy responded in agreement but said that when the bill collectors keep calling she thinks about it, "But somebody would find out." Nancy and her family do not have a car that is running and no money to get either car fixed. The family doesn't go out to eat or for any type of entertainment because there isn't money. Were Nancy to separate from Chad, she could receive full AFDC, educational training, government supported child care and transportation coverage.

Dreams for the Future

Nancy responded: "Raising and supporting my kids and having enough for food and clothes—I'm behind on everything." Terry responded: "Starting school and maybe making enough to buy my own home." Family themes for the Cyclers' lives included *Rosanne* for Nancy and for Terry *I Love Lucy*.

Group Three: Combiners

"The kids love to go to McDonald's but it doesn't fill them up and the kids want extra burgers."

Combiners piggyback a combination of earned income and some form of supplementation because their earnings are inadequate and/or unpredictable. In order to be classified as a Combiner a family must have been working for a minimum of one year, receive some form of supplementation from relatives or the government, and not be receiving

AFDC. This group's major concerns are low wages, low education, and lack of benefits, especially health care, from their employers. Combiners at one time may have been Self Sufficient or even Welfare Dependent but have now had a corresponding upward or downward change in earnings which has led to a combined reliance on earned income, coupled with government assistance and/or, in some cases, kinship assistance.

The profile of the Combiner is based on thirteen cases from the study. Four of the Combiners work; the others are dependent upon a male wage earner. Three of the employed women are not married, while the fourth is. This family is the only dual earner Combiner, and the woman in this family works only part-time. The other married Combiners are full-time homemakers, often by choice. All of their husbands are employed. These married couple families net between $750 to $1,550 per month while the female headed Combiner families net between $800 and $1,200 per month. The two lowest earning male partners are segregated in nonmanual service positions while the other highest earning male partners who are concentrated in manual labor positions net over $1,000 a month. Four Combiners supplement their income with housing or food stamps. They receive an average of $275 in government assistance. Other Combiners would qualify for assistance but instead choose to be self-reliant with the assistance of relatives at the present time. Three Combiners live in homes that were paid for by relatives or have paid them off themselves; one receives a government housing subsidy.

Demographics
In contrast to the first two groups, none of the Combiners' parents relied on government assistance.[1] The average age at which a Combiner first became a parent was 19 years old; the oldest being 24 and the youngest 17. Their age at first birth compares favorably with the Welfare Dependent group for whom the average age at first birth was 18.5 years. A Combiner was married in most cases when she first began to parent. Three of the five African American Combiners were unmarried. Combiners generally, however, were unmarried at first birth only around one-fourth of the time compared to over three–fourths and four-fifths of the time among Cyclers and Welfare Dependent, respectively. Her ethnicity varies; she is European American in eight cases and African

American in five cases. She has an average of 2.8 children. This group consists today of predominately married couples (77 percent) who are traditionally classified as working poor, compared to the first two groups who are predominately female headed families. What follows is the Combiners story.

The Combiner is on the average 30.5 years old today. It has been around eleven-and-one-half years since she first gave birth at age 19. The major reasons for combining wages with supplemental kinship or government assistance are low wages or seasonal work. Supplementation generally takes two forms, namely, government food stamp subsidies and independent, but kinship-subsidized housing, often on family land. The following quotes from Sue, Judy, Martha and other Combiners illustrate the life experiences associated with this type of poverty in the United States. Sue, whose case study is highlighted in this section, supplements her family income through kinship aid as does Judy; Martha supplements hers with food stamps.

Sue, a European American, is 26 years old. She has two children; they are ages one and five. Both children are from the same partner, Cary, whom she has been with for six-and-one-half years. They decided to marry when she became pregnant with her first child. Sue and Cary live on her family's land in a mobile home that she received from her parents. Her parents and a sister also live in trailers on the same land. Cary is a long distance truck driver and is on the road five days a week, leaving Sue to manage the house. He brings home around $350 per week without benefits. She wants to go back to work but has not worked since the birth of their first child. She feels *stuck* at home with little money and also little opportunity for employment in a rural area. Sue's life experiences are highlighted in the illustrations below, along with Judy, Martha and others'.

While Growing Up With My Family
Only two of the women who are Combiners were raised in female headed households as teens, compared to two-thirds of the women in the previous two groups. Only one Combiner's family received government assistance while growing up, and then, only rarely. Often the women's fathers worked in upper level manual positions such as assembly production or

in high wage service positions such as sales and teaching. About half the women's mothers worked in upper level manual assembly work or low wage secretarial positions and the other half were homemakers. The average number of children in the home while growing up was 4.1. The largest family had 11 children; they were rural working poor and never received government assistance. Three Combiners rated their housing while growing up as crowded or overcrowded and the others rated theirs as comfortable or spacious. The average age at which the Combiners' sisters first gave birth was 19.9 years old. This was considerably older than the first two groups. Their sisters are currently working in areas such as banking, health care and assembly. Sue, the rural Combiner introduced earlier, remembered early family life this way:

> "There were three boys and myself in the family when I was growing up. My stepfather was a shipping clerk and my mother was a welder. We lived in a mobile home in the country; it was really crowded. My parents never had any government assistance."

Judy is the youngest of the women I interviewed. She is only 24. Her parents have never been on government assistance and she has regular contact with them. In fact, her son stays with Grandma each weekend. Judy stated:

> "It is a time that Grandma cherishes and it gives me and Sam, [her husband] time out." Judy has one brother and no sisters. "My mother is a homemaker—just like I am." Judy chooses not to work, even part-time, while the children are young even though they could really use the money. While growing up her father provided the income. He worked in a manual position as an assembly worker. Judy's husband, Sam, has a high school education. Sam is working for Hertz car rental and "is really excited about it after having piece-meal jobs for three years of *tough times.*" He will get hospitalization and vacation after one year and is hoping he can eventually move up. Sam makes $5.25 per hour. This is the highest income ever earned in this young

couple's life. Their perception at this point is that they are *doing well* after three years of trying to get off to a good start. She is using contraception so they won't have the desired second child until they can afford it.

Sexual Activity

The median age at which Combiners began sexual activity was 16, the average age for the other women in the study. The next most frequent ages they mentioned were 17, then 15. The most common place in which sexual activity occurred was in the parent's home, either his or hers, which is again consistent with the other women in the study. The second most often reported location in which sexual activity took place was another relative's home, then their boyfriend's home. Menstrual periods most frequently occurred at age twelve or an average of four years before the women engaged in sexual activity. Around one-half did not use contraception; around one-half did, although not always correctly. Among those Combiners who did not use contraception only two women, including Sue, reported wanting to have a child. Three women did not really think about it one way or the other and two reported not wanting a child, but were not taking appropriate measures in order to prevent it. For the two women who wanted to have a child, the time interval between first engaging in sexual activity and pregnancy was considerably longer than for others in the group, three or more years. For those Combiners who reported not wanting a child at that time, but were not using contraception, the time interval until pregnancy was as short as one month, but averaged only four to six months. Some women were just unlucky in the timing of their sexual activity, regardless of their desire or ambivalence toward having a baby and regardless of the frequency of coital practice. Lisa and Carmen, illustrated this experience. Lisa reported:

They met when she was 15 and he was 16. Both were virgins the first time they had sex and she got pregnant that first time. They married and now have four children. Carmen had sex for the first time two weeks before her 18th birthday because of peer pressure from her friends to do so before she turned 18. She wishes she could go back and do things differently, but sees such mistakes we make as "part of how we grow in life." Both of her kids are from the same man and are three years apart. Carmen dated Barry for eight years. When they began having sex she got pregnant within four to six months but kept having her periods. She found out she was pregnant when she became dehydrated and went to the doctor. She and Barry did not use contraception. "He said he knew what he was doing." The fourth time they had sex she got pregnant. Carmen was on birth control with her second child by him but still got pregnant. "I would do it differently if I could go back. I hope my kids will learn from my past."

Among the contraceptive-using Combiners, such as Sue, sexual activity began at around the same time as with non-contraceptive users, age 16. Sue stopped using contraception after one-and-a-half years in order to have a child. The others who used contraception differed from Sue; they had unplanned pregnancies that occurred on average one year after initiating sexual activity, often because of inaccurate or inconsistent contraceptive usage. Thus, some of those who used contraceptives weren't very "lucky" either, as these cases illustrate:

Sam got pregnant the first time she had sex. They started using condoms and a sponge right after that but she had already gotten pregnant and didn't know. She was scared to tell anyone. Sam finally told her mom, "I had the *throw'n up flu.* "As a result, Sam did not have prenatal care and she delivered two weeks later.

With Judy's first sexual partner, Bill, she used condoms that he provided and did not get pregnant. When she started going with Mike she was going to get on the pill, "but I got pregnant before I got around to it." She was living at her parents at the time, then she and Mike moved in together. They were scheduled to be married on the day the baby came, but he arrived early. So they waited for two weeks.

Even when using contraception regularly, it is not fail proof as can be seen in Sherrie's situation:

> "I was on the pill when I got pregnant". She took it every day, but "didn't take it right." When I asked what she meant, Sherrie said, "Like at the same time every day." Her mother encouraged her to get married when she found out she was pregnant. Sherrie was 18 at the time. They were married for ten years but subsequently divorced.

Intimate Relationships
Over three-fourths of Combiners were married by the time they gave birth, regardless of whether the pregnancy was planned or unplanned. Three of the women who were married at first birth and one who married later subsequently divorced. Three women who were divorced from their first partners eventually remarried; the other did not. It is interesting to note that the three African American Combiners who were unmarried at first birth are the only women in the group who are currently not married (one did eventually marry but is currently unmarried). Some of the women schemed to marry without their partners' knowledge:

> Sue, the rural homemaker introduced in the case study, stopped taking the pill without her boyfriend's knowledge so she could get pregnant and have her boyfriend, now her husband, marry her. In one sense Sue got what she wanted, but she is not happy. They have been married five years and now have two children. However, when I asked what was her biggest concern for the future, she replied, "Whether to stay with the father of my children who I am no longer in love with." Sue's biggest relationship concern is that her husband wants to have sex and she no longer wants to. "Today, I can not stand the thought of sleeping with him; it's just not there anymore. The wolf (pet) doesn't like Cary. So when I don't want him to be near me, I let the wolf in bed and then he doesn't come close."

Martha, another Combiner whom I would like to introduce, is very happy with her husband whom she met when she ran away from home at 18. Martha reported:

"I ran away at 18 and met Ricky while I was hitch-hiking to California. I was into drugs and was screwing a lot of men when I met him. We went out to California together and got help from another Cuban family out there. These people did not want Ricky and me to stay at their house unless we were married. So we got married after knowing each other only two months. I got pregnant after four months. We've now been married for 16 years and have been off drugs for eight."

Lisa is also happy. She is with her second partner; she was married to the first for 12 years. She and John have lived together for over seven years. Lisa's biggest relationship issue is that she has never been able to decide whether or not to marry. They have two children. John owns a body shop and pays the bills, although she too has always worked.

Education and Employment
Twelve Combiners had not completed high school when they first conceived. Eight were still in high school and three had already dropped out before they became pregnant. Of the eight who were still in high school, five graduated between the time of conception and delivery. The other three did not remain in school. They dropped out within one year of the birth. One of these women, Tamara, whose story is illustrated below, returned to school within a year. The second woman, Tammy, tried to remain in school after her child was born but quit within the year. She eventually acquired a GED eight years later. Most recently Tammy received a certificate from Vo-Tech as a medical technician because AFDC regulations required her to return to school. Tammy has never been employed in the field in which she received training and is a full-time homemaker. Their current source of income is her husband's net earnings of $1,000 per month, with no additional government subsidies. Indeed, no women who were required by AFDC to return to school are currently

employed in the field of that training. The third woman who conceived while in high school and did not remain in school, never returned to complete her education. It has been twelve years but she hopes to eventually receive a GED. She, too, is married and a full-time homemaker. Tamara relayed the following story:

> She left school after completing her junior year while pregnant with her first child. Coincidentally, it is because she got pregnant for a second time a year later that she was able to complete her education. She took advantage of a child care program the high school had initiated for pregnant mothers. However, the program only covers the year of the pregnancy; after that, the women are on their own to find suitable child care for any subsequent years of schooling.

The other five Combiners were not in school at the time of their first pregnancy. Three women had dropped out of high school prior to conceiving; the others had graduated. Those who did not graduate completed the 9th, 10th and 11th grades. (One of them returned after her abortion and received a GED before the first birth.) Two women who dropped out were already married at first birth. Sue, the rural homemaker who got pregnant without her boyfriend's knowledge already graduated. from high school. She reported:

> "I was out of high school when I became pregnant even though the school I had attended was ranked second in the nation in teen pregnancies." After conceiving her first child and marrying, Sue was attending Litten business school when she became pregnant with her second child. The doctor made her stay in bed for four months because of bleeding. "They kicked me out (of business school)." Sue and her husband, Cary, are trying to get back $8,000 in tuition she paid or at least not be liable for the rest she owes.

Employment

There are three currently unmarried women who are Combiners and are supporting their families. They are classified as working poor. There are ten married Combiners. The three female headed working poor are worse off when comparing available net income, minus housing and child care costs. It is not that they earn less than the other women in the study, nor is it because the married couples are dual earners, but because the men of the married couple families generally have greater earning power. This is because of occupational segregation into manual versus service positions, largely on the basis of gender. The female headed Combiner's average available income after subtracting housing and any child care costs is $535 per month. Only two of the male-based Combiner families fare as poorly as the female-based. Moreover, the poorest of the male-based are comparable to the most well off of the female-based. Generally speaking, the available income for women who are full-time homemakers and rely on a male's earnings is considerably higher. Their available income, minus housing and child care costs (no child care since the women are full-time homemakers), averages $1,045 per month or double that of the female-based single earner Combiners.

Gay, one of the female-based Combiners, discussed the consequences of low wages employment:

> Gay sees herself as a teacher. She taught at a Montessori school for several years but it closed down without notice because of financial hardship as a result of its proximity to the Oklahoma City bombing. Gay is now working at another day care center, but gets only $5.00 an hour instead of the $7.00 she once earned. Gay receives no subsidies, pays her own rent, and wants to be fully independent. She will get health benefits after a few months and that will be a big help but the two dollar an hour pay cut she recently took because of losing the other teaching position makes a big difference in what she can give her daughter. She stated, "I have enough to pay the bills but not to do the other things I would like to do for Rachele." Gay has been working since two weeks after Rachele was born. She is now seven. Gay wanted to take care of her daughter and give her

enough to make up for not having a father in her life. However, she is worried that by the time she gets home at night and gets cleaned up that there isn't enough time left over in the day to spend with her daughter. Gay asked what I thought; it was difficult to answer.

Some of the married couples are not much better off, especially when the husbands are segregated in low wage, nonunion manual positions without benefits:

Martha, the former drug user whom you met earlier, and her husband live in a house that they bought for $3,500 at an auction. As previously mentioned, Martha met her husband at 18 when she left home and was hitch-hiking to California. They married on the road. Several years later Ricky lost his job as a diesel mechanic. He had car trouble and could not get to work for three days. Ricky was fired. Because he was from Cuba, people would ask him for drugs, so he started dealing. During some months he and his wife made over $5,000 selling cocaine. He now makes $5.05 an hour. Ricky and Martha were both busted for dealing drugs and he went to jail for two years. Ricky's asylum status is now in question because of his drug felony. He now has to renew his work card every six months at a cost of $70 (a lot for this family to come up with) even though it has been eight years since he was in prison. Ricky currently works as a custodian at the church they now attend.

Government and Kinship Assistance

The biggest problems Combiners face are housing and health care costs, both of which can be subsidized by the government, but not at the income levels of most Combiners. In order to qualify for housing assistance, 50 percent of one's income must go to pay for housing (Personal communication: Oklahoma Housing Authority). The homeless and those living in shelters receive first priority. This is why one of the interviewees strategized to live at the Jesus House at the time of her first birth; she could then get into assisted housing without the average three year wait. The housing eligibility requirements essentially eliminate anyone already earning over $800 a month, and living independently, thereby making government subsidized housing unavailable to most working poor.

Many Combiners or working poor are in a Catch-22 situation. They earn too much for government assisted housing and health care, yet do not earn enough to compensate for these expenses. Often housing and health care use up most of their earnings. So, many devise informal networks and strategies to make ends meet, often combining kinship, government and earned income for much of their lives. Sue, whose story was highlighted at the beginning of the section on Combiners, juggled housing costs this way:

> Sue, her husband and kids live in a trailer on the family land on which she had grown up. There was at least one other trailer, which probably belonged to her sister, her parent's trailer, and Sue's. "We were looking for an apartment, to get away from the closed-in feeling of living so close to my parents but I'm not sure how soon, if at all, it will happen." Sue is a full–time homemaker. She had one in diapers which I held during part of the interview. The place was pretty run down but the rent was free and the kids could play on the acreage that would not be available in an apartment. Although the family provided a friendship and mutual aid support network, Sue said she felt isolated. ". . .with my husband on the road as an oil field worker (with whom she no longer is intimate) and living on the outskirts of town and not much money left over." While I was there a call came about an overdue bill with Color Tile. They were faithfully paying on it each month and she promised a payment when Cary got in from the road midweek.

Another of the Combiners expressed her health care and other financial concerns this way:

> When I arrived at Lisa's apartment in Farmington, it was clean and Lisa was waiting for me. We sat at the dining room table and talked. The aroma from a pleasant future evening meal was simmering on the stove. When I asked what was cooking, she

responded, "it's neck bones." I smiled thinking of my vegetarian cuisine that was so different from Lisa's and yet we prepare both meals with love and to nourish those whom we love. Lisa said, The kids love to go to McDonald's but it doesn't fill them up and the kids want extra burgers. The other day her daughter wanted to go so bad, but she had to tell her, "we don't have the money to go but someday we will have." When I asked Lisa her dream for her future years, she responded, "It's to take the kids out to eat a hamburger like all their friends get to do." I am reminded of the wonderful smell of the neck bones simmering on her stove when I think of the working poor. Her husband, Jerome, has worked construction for the same company for seven years and earns $8.00 an hour to support his family of six, including his wife of eleven years. Lisa's medicine for Lupus and diabetes cost them $300 per month out of his $8.00 an hour earnings. If Lisa and her husband separated, her medication would be fully covered by Medicaid.

In addition to housing and health care costs, a common difficulty faced by the Combiners and others who are poor is the time-lag between applying for benefits and receiving them while living on meager earnings. Many women told of having a sudden drop in income because of a job change or loss, then waiting nearly two months before seeing an appropriate change in their subsidies. In addition, the women told of the difficulty, expenditure of time, and burdensome paperwork required of them every three months in order to maintain their government subsidies. If an individual missed the time to renew or did not have the appropriate documentation, women reported losing coverage for one to three months before the paperwork caught up. Nevertheless, the assistance received in government subsidies can make the difference in whether a family can stay above the poverty level as Judy and others informed me:

Judy and her husband applied for AFDC when he was doing odd jobs but they did not qualify. They did qualify for stamps and received them for about three years after he was fired from his job. They are still getting them. "It helps out a lot." Judy's family receives $170 in stamps in addition to her husband's earnings of $840 per month, boosting their income by about 20 percent on a monthly basis.

Jennifer had this to say. Mike's work is seasonal and he receives no benefits. He and Jennifer have received stamps for six years. The kids are covered by Medicaid, but Jennifer is not. Her husband is covered by Indian health services but again, Jennifer is not. "We're trying to get the kids on it (Indian health services) but the paperwork is hard to understand and the telephone number to get questions answered is long distance." She and Mike have spent $20 (a lot of money to them) on calls. Even though they are his children they have to prove their heritage back to 1906 using birth and marriage documents.

Pam is one of many poor women who devised strategies in order to receive Medicaid because her husband does not have medical coverage at work. Actually he can receive coverage at work if he pays for it. For their family it would cost over $50 of his weekly pay, so they only carry accidental that runs them $15 per month. Medicaid will cover the kids for about one year, she said. After that she has to devise strategies. Pam said, "I have to find a disability and get the kids on SSI in order to get coverage (medical) for them." Otherwise, they are not eligible for Medicaid unless the family pays the first $1000. One child is on SSI and receives $512 per month and another child's case is pending, both for Attention Deficit Disorder.

Support Networks

Lynn mentioned that when she needs to chill out, her husband watches the kids in the evening and she goes to a club and then comes back refreshed. On the weekend the whole family was going canoeing down the Illinois river.

Tammy goes to a friend's house just to talk; they exchange errands as well. The kids have regular contact with her brother and their paternal grandparents. Their father, her ex–husband, sees them at least once a week. As for her, she juggles work, family and school, as well as being a wife.

Judy said her mother showed her how to rear a child. "For the first two weeks I was overprotective and was afraid to say (for example) clean her nose for fear I would hurt her. But, her mother showed her how to ". . . burp her, when to feed and how much, and how to keep her clean and warm."

Dreams for the Future

To supplement their income, Pam has primarily worked in the fast food industry. Her major goal at this point is to finish college. Her Bachelor's degree will be in Elementary Education. Pell grants have enabled her to get this far. She has finished an Associate's degree.

Tammy, her three kids and husband live in a condo they are buying. As with many in urban areas today, they live behind closed security fences and their children play in a cement jungle or in the house. She concurred with another woman I interviewed the day before, when she said, "We are the prisoners today, living behind fences and afraid to look another in the face or go out of our locked house in the night."

Carmen works full-time but lives in HUD housing. She pays $175 of the rent and the rest is covered by government assistance. The home decor is black and white with glass accents. I still remember that her dining table looked as though it was from a magazine—with the linens in the glasses, just waiting for some imaginary lover to join her for dinner—she hopes to meet one some day.

Group Four: Temporary Poverty

"I was on stamps but as soon as I got a raise (to $7.00 an hour) they cut me off the stamps."

The category of Temporary Poverty refers to women who have been in poverty for a single period of up to five years and have subsequently been self-sufficient for a period of at least one year. It is possible that some of these women may be Cyclers and are just entering their first period of being off government assistance and will cycle back into poverty as new life challenges arise. The difference between the women in Temporary Poverty and the Combiners is that these women do not currently rely on any type of government assistance and are self-supporting. They may rely on occasional Medicaid coverage for pregnancy if they or their spouses do not have coverage with their employers. Temporarily poor women differ from those who are Welfare Dependent because they have been off government assistance for a period of at least one year. This sustained period of self-sufficiency, rather than a few weeks, was thought to be a better indicator of a true temporary period of poverty that is less likely to be repeated.

Demographics

This profile is based on eleven cases from the study. The net income ranges from $500 to $1,500 per month for the women in this group. All the male spouses of women in the Temporary Poverty category are currently employed. Their net income ranges from $840 to $2,400 per month. On average the male partners earn 30 percent more than the women. In two cases, women in Temporary Poverty live in homes that are paid for, so they do not have a house payment. The others are paying rent or a mortgage out of their earned income.

In two situations the women in Temporary Poverty's parents relied on government assistance. The average age at which the women in temporary poverty became parents was 20, the oldest was 21 and the youngest 16. While this is not considerably different than the rest of the sample, it is nevertheless much younger than for the general public. The women have an average of 2.8 children. Most of the women who experienced a period of temporary poverty were married at first birth. The women in Temporary Poverty were unmarried at first birth in only 18 percent of the cases. This is considerably less frequently than the first three groups who were unmarried as often as 88 percent of the time (group one). The women in Temporary Poverty are all European American; whereas the women in group one were all African American. This group also consists predominately of women who are currently married but vary greatly in their present economic situation. They also vary greatly in the reasons they were among the 40 percent of Americans who experience a dip into poverty at some point in their lives. What follows is the story of the married couple and female headed women in Temporary Poverty.

The reasons for entering and exiting poverty varied for the women who experienced a temporary period of poverty. The major reasons they entered poverty were because of a separation or divorce, low income, not working, or leaving a job to care for relatives. The reasons the women cited for exiting poverty were because of acquiring a better paying job, starting to work, marriage, or moving in with a partner. This group of women is on average 30 years old, an average of ten years since they first gave birth at age twenty. These women are remarkably similar in current age and time since first birth to the other groups, yet they are no longer poor. The following quotes from Heather, Randy and other women who were temporarily poor illustrate the differing life experiences associated with this type of poverty in the United States. Heather was Welfare Dependent until she married; whereas Randy was Welfare Dependent until she began working. Let us first turn to the story of Heather.

Heather, a European American, is 27 years old. She has two children ages seven and nine. Each child is from a separate partner to whom she was never married. She has been with her husband, Brad, for four-and-a-half years. He currently brings home $1,000 per month as a technician; she brings home $485 per month as a child care worker. The deed to their home is in her husband's name because he owned it before they were married. The mortgage is $296 per month. Heather's story is highlighted in the illustrations below along with Randy's and others.

While Growing Up With My Family

Only two of the Temporary Poverty women were raised in female headed households as teens. This is comparable to the Combiners; whereas, the majority (two-thirds) of the Welfare Dependent and Cyclers were raised in female headed households. The fathers of the Temporary Poverty women generally worked in upper level manual positions such as assembly and trucking, or in high wage service positions as supervisors and small business owners. Most of the women's mothers were employed; only two were full-time homemakers. Around half of the women who were temporarily poor had mothers who worked in low wage nonmanual positions such as retail and clerical. The other employed mothers worked in manual labor positions as cooks and assembly line workers. The average number of siblings was 3.3, but several of the Temporary Poverty women had only one sibling. Two of the women in this group were raised in extended families. In such families it was often the grandparents rather than the parents who provided current kinship aid. Four of the Temporary Poverty women rated their housing while growing up as crowded, none as overcrowded. The majority of the women rated theirs as comfortable or spacious. The average age at which the sisters of the women in Temporary Poverty first gave birth was quite young, 18.5 years old. That was nearly one-and-a-half years younger than the sisters of the Combiners, but the same age as the sisters of the Welfare Dependent. The Temporary Poverty women's sisters are currently working in areas such as clerical, health care and fast food.

Heather, whose case study is featured in this section, did not have a happy life as a teenager as she discusses below; whereas, Randy did and continues to have close contact with her parents today. Randy mentioned:

"My mother was a homemaker and my father worked at Tinker. We were never on assistance while growing up and lived in the same house my whole life. I have two sisters; one got pregnant at 16 but today she works as a nurse. I have to borrow money from Mom and Dad once and awhile to make my bills but I always try to pay it back."

Heather, on the other hand remembers this about her childhood. She stated:

"I was kicked out at age 14. I lived with my mom before that and she didn't pay much attention to what I did. She (mom) drank. I started having sex when I was 10; he was 18."

Another woman in Temporary Poverty illustrated the importance of the extended kinship network for some women living in poverty. Robin is currently living with her grandparents. During the interview, she mused:

They were a close rural extended family network. Robin was staying with her grandparents after having just gotten married only one week earlier. Her brother's wife watched her kids while Robin worked during the day and then they all came to the grandparents for a big family meal. I felt welcome with a continually filled cup of coffee and lots of conversation with Grandma. She was in the kitchen cooking as Robin and I sat at the table and talked. Grandpa was close by in the living room playing with the grand kids and pulling stems from grapes for jelly.

Sexual Activity

The median age at which the women in the Temporary Poverty group began sexual activity was 16 which is consistent with the other women in the study. The next most frequent ages at which coitus began were 17, then 15. Two women engaged in voluntary sex quite early, one of whom was Heather whose case study was introduced earlier. She began at 10, another woman at 13; whereas, Randy began at the median age of 16. The most common place in which sexual activity occurred was in their parent's homes, either the women's or her boyfriend's. All groups of women in the study engaged in sexual activity in their parents' homes the majority of the time. The second most frequent location for sexual activity was another relative's home, a car, and then the woman's own home. Menstrual periods for the women in Temporary Poverty most frequently began at age twelve, as was the case for most women in the study. The women reported an interval ranging from immediately to seven years between the onset of menses and engaging in sexual activity. Once the temporarily poor women began having sexual relations, they engaged in sexual activity from 10 times a month to only twice a year.

One-third of the women in this group did not use contraception. The others used condoms or birth control pills. Those women using condoms, such as Randy, tended to use them from one-fourth to three-fourths of the time, but never all the time. Of the five women using birth control pills, four, including Heather, had an unplanned pregnancy. The pregnancies occurred because they ran out of pills, were changing brands, or did not take it correctly. In other words, only one woman using birth control had a planned pregnancy; the others were not using contraception consistently or their contraceptive practice failed. This led many of them into a period of temporary poverty. The non-contraceptive users reported that they, "did not really think about it (pregnancy) one way or the other." The average length of time between becoming sexually active and first pregnancy ranged from the first month to three years. One of the women who did not use contraception had this to say during the interview:

"We did it about ten times a month, usually at one of our parent's houses while they were at work. I did not use contraception back then." Sherrie reported that when she asked Harry about it he said not to worry he would withdraw in time. "He said he would pull it out so I wouldn't get pregnant." Sherrie got pregnant within one month. She and Harry initiated sexual activity in the summer and Sherrie had her first child the following March while still a junior in high school. They were both 16. She had her period the first few months. Sherrie didn't tell her mother until she went to the emergency room to deliver, thus having no prenatal care. By the following year and the birth of their second child at age 17, they were married. They were living with Sherrie's mother. Her mother passed away during this pregnancy and the landlord made Sherrie and her new husband move because they were both underage. Today, Sherrie works as a hair dresser and is self-sufficient. She and Harry are divorced.

Heather, who was introduced earlier, had her first sexual experience at 10 with a boy of 18. At age 14 she was kicked out of the house, then ran away and lived on her own. Heather's mother was an alcoholic and did not provide any parental supervision. After Heather left home she worked her way from McDonald's to McDonald's under an assumed name. When a manager would ask her to remember to bring in an ID, she would move on. "The biggest problem" she stated, "was when people called me Georgia Brusher (her fake name) and I would forget to respond." Her mother reported to the police that Heather had run away. At one point she was put in a group home. That event was a turning point is her life. The shelter staff helped her to get a GED and find her first apartment. Sherrie had quit school when she left home at 14.

A major problem many of the Temporary Poverty women and others in the study faced is the postponement of receiving health care because they could not afford its cost and were not covered by other medical insurance. Another problem was that the women were not seen by the same physician regularly. A final problem was the loss of jobs during pregnancy because of health complications. In the first illustration, Heather's experiences during pregnancy highlight the problems faced by women in poverty when pregnant. Another woman, in the subsequent illustration, also demonstrates the difficulties women bear during pregnancy:

Heather had her period during all four of her miscarriages and was on the pill the entire time. The father of the fetuses, Mike, lived at the homeless shelter with Heather. She reported that the doctors were trying to get her birth control pills straightened out and kept changing them around. One fetus was dead for two months inside Heather and she had carried it for three months live. Heather was bleeding and the doctor thought it was her appendix. Had she not passed it, Heather reported that she would have died from the toxins. When Heather and Mike conceived again, she was working at Little Ceasars. The doctors ordered her to quit work and have bed rest. She did not go back to work afterwards because her daughter was so sick with asthma. Heather stayed home to care for her. By this time she was living on her own, no longer involved with Mike, and Welfare Dependent.

All Sally can remember is wanting to get married and raise kids; she wanted six. Her first husband owes $15,000 in back child support and can afford to pay it. He owns a sign company and does well. They did not have insurance at the time of their first child, so they made payments to cover the cost of the delivery. They also made payments to cover the cost of the second child, since being in business for himself, they had no insurance coverage. Sally said, "It almost broke us." She had to quit work with her second child because of problems with the pregnancy. The baby was turned backward and, under doctors orders, she had to stay in bed. Sally never went back to her job. Today, Sally is remarried and works part-time.

Intimate Relationships
All but two women in Temporary Poverty were married by the time they first gave birth, even though only one pregnancy was planned. Later in life, all but one subsequently divorced. This group has the largest number of women who were married at first birth of the four groups discussed thus far. Over three-fourths of the women are also married or remarried today. Only four are presently divorced or were never married. For the women of Temporary Poverty, the reason they are not in poverty today is not that they were married at first birth, but that they have remarried or remained married later in life. Linda is an example of those women whose lives demonstrate the relationship between marriage and poverty. She and her family today would be classified as rural working poor:

She got married on her 18th birthday. Alan was her first sexual partner. They had sex only one time before they got married. They had known each other 13 months when their first child was born. Linda said, "We separated for about three years just after we got married. During that period AFDC made me return to school or be dropped. I went to Vo-tech for mechanic's training. I never used the training and am a full-time homemaker." She and Alan have been together 15 years.

Randy has never been married. She explained:

"I started screwing at 16 and was with several men. I got pregnant during a one night stand. I got pregnant again at 17 and lived with him for awhile, but he beat me. I decided to give that child up for adoption. I kept my first child and she is the joy of my life." Randy is now 22, has her GED, and works full–time to support herself and her six–year–old daughter. She'd like to marry someday but, "I never want to be involved with someone who beats me again."

Education and Employment

Five women in Temporary Poverty compared to twelve Combiners had not completed high school when they first conceived. Seven women were no longer in high school and were working at the time of their pregnancy. About half quit, either during or shortly after delivery, because of health complications, kinship obligations, or moves. Among those who did not complete high school, Heather dropped out before becoming pregnant. Randy and another woman quit school around the time of their pregnancies or shortly after delivery. The other two women who conceived during high school graduated between the time of conception and delivery. The three women who dropped out were able to complete a GED, two because of AFDC requirements and assistance, and the other because of child care assistance from relatives. Linda, the rural working poor woman introduced earlier, was one of those who conceived while in high school:

It was Linda's senior year when she got pregnant but she managed to graduate by the time her child was born. After his birth, she and Alan separated for a time. AFDC required her to go to school during that time or be dropped from the program, so she went to Vo-Tech for mechanic's training. Linda has never worked in the field in which she received training and does not intend to. She has never worked except for running an informal day care center in her home while Alan is at work. She also sometimes cleans houses under the table so that no taxes are taken out.

Corrine has worked at least part–time most of her adult life, mainly at fast food places. She now works at Kmart and her husband, Glen, is doing custom paint work for a car dealer. He just started, but may soon get hospitalization. She hopes that it comes through. The kids are fully covered on Medicaid right now because of their parent's low earnings. Corrine took a business course which she said was useless because, "Everywhere I applied wanted experience." Corrine and her husband, Glen, are currently studying at a regional university; she hopes to be a forensic specialist.

Government and Kinship Assistance

As mentioned earlier, the biggest obstacles for those who were in a temporary period of poverty and are now struggling to be self-sufficient are low wages and lack, or high cost of, medical coverage now that they are employed. Pamela's experiences reflect this struggle:

She was on Medicaid for the pregnancy only. They would not cover her afterwards because she has asthma. As a result Pamela has eight years of hospital bills between $2,000 to $3,000 per visit for her asthma attacks. She and her husband have been slowly paying on them, a little at a time, for eight years. They now have medical coverage because Chuck is receiving benefits as a machine operator.

Whereas Pamela received Medicaid while pregnant, others, such as Sherrie, do not even qualify for medical coverage during their pregnancies.

> The wedding occurred just one week after her mom died. It was a terrible time for Harry and Sherrie. They did not have insurance so they had to pay cash for the delivery. Sherrie used what was left of the life insurance policy from her mother's death to pay for the baby's delivery. The doctor requested payment by the seventh month of the pregnancy or he would not continue to see her. The hospital allowed them to make payments. They made too much at their jobs to qualify for Medicaid but did not earn enough to cover hospital expenses without going into debt. To make matters worse both Harry and Sherrie were still in high school.

With each raise the working poor receive in their employment, government subsidies are reduced and eventually withdrawn, thereby creating both a work disincentive and a reinforcement of their poverty position. At certain levels the drop in benefits exceeds the increase from the employer, leaving the women and their families poorer than before. Randy, a single mother, expressed this frustration:

> "I was on housing until I turned 21, then they cut me off because I started working. I made $4.85 an hour. I still get child care assistance. My co-payment is $6.00 a month. But with my next raise (probably 25 cents), my co-payment will go up $20.00 per month."

Another of the women's experiences concurs with Randy's:

> "I was on stamps, but as soon as I got a raise (to $7.00 an hour) they cut me off the stamps."

Other critical issues for those who were once poor and are struggling to remain self-sufficient include reliable transportation and child care. In some cases, without one or both, it is not economically advantageous for a woman to work, especially if she is married and they can survive on his income. The unmarried women have little choice in these matters. Randy's situation exemplifies the problems of child care and transportation:

> She lives in a pretty run down apartment and is proud to be paying the entire rent on her own, without the aid of the government or relatives. It is quite dark inside, yet she has many special treasures set about. The apartment is surrounded by concrete and a parking lot which is the only play area for her daughter. Randy lives here because it's affordable and is next to the fast food place where she works. Randy cannot drive because she has epilepsy. Her mother assists with child care because the day care is not always open during the times Randy works.

Many women who do not receive subsidized day care must pay the expense from their meager earnings. Corrine stated:

> Her mother is the baby sitter when they need one. They pay her between $50 to $100 per month to sit when their combined work and school schedules interfere. "It is still a lot cheaper than a day care or regular baby sitter," Corrine said.

Temporary Poverty Periods and Government Assistance
Women who have experienced a temporary period of poverty generally fall into two categories that have differing types of life histories. First are those women such as Heather and Randy who were Welfare Dependent for an extended period but are now self-reliant because of stable employment, as in Randy's case, or because of marriage, as in Heather's case. The second category is those women who experienced a shorter period of poverty because of job loss, illness, or injury and are once again re-employed. Both types of Temporary Poverty situations are illustrated below. First we return to Heather's story and then we meet Lilian.

Heather became Welfare Dependent with the birth of her first child at age 20, while living at the homeless shelter. She quit work at that time and did not go back until three years later, after the birth of her second child. She was single for both births and on full government benefits, including housing. Heather eventually married and is now completely off government assistance, but is now husband-reliant. Both she and her husband work full-time but she only clears $500 per month. Heather has shifted from being *Welfare Dependent* to *Husband Dependent*. Should they divorce, Heather would once again be on welfare, given her present earning power, unless she receives additional training which she has no plans to do. Her husband earns around $1,000 a month after deductions, including $60.00 a month for health insurance. The house they live in was his before they married. Should they divorce the house is his.

Lilian was on assistance one time for seven months and never again. She was on assistance while her husband was in jail for drinking and driving. During that period Lilian was able to cover the bills but had to plan and budget. For example, she stated, "The family loves pork steaks but I couldn't afford to buy them while on assistance."

Dreams for the Future

Randy has to move because her landlord is making her. She hopes someday to be able to afford to own a house and have her epilepsy regulated to the point where she can drive.

Heather would like to have a house in the country, one which she feels is her own because the one they currently live in was her husband's before they met. Her final hope is to get through the teen years with her kids because, "it's a tough world out there."

Group Five: Self Sufficient

"If I get sick I wait to see if I get over it. For the kids, I have an uncle who is a pediatrician and prescribes if it's simple or we go to a private physician and make payments."

The category of Self Sufficient refers to women who rely on only Medicaid or no type of government or kinship assistance. To be included in this category, a woman's reliance on government assistance, if at all, would have been limited to pregnancy and then a return to self sufficiency. In one instance, a female did not receive any assistance even during pregnancy. She delivered at the Oklahoma Memorial Hospital Women's Clinic and therefore was recruited to participate in the study. She went to the clinic for this delivery because she had previously delivered stillborn twins there and received excellent care. Most of the women, however, attended this clinic because of their reliance on Medicaid.

The primary reason that women in this category relied on government assistance is that they or their partners did not have medical coverage through their employers. The period of medical coverage began when prenatal care was initiated and generally continued through delivery and the infant's first checkups and immunizations. The period of medical coverage among the Self Sufficient women ranged between six months and one year, depending on when obstetrical care began. The shortest reported period was six months, the longest was one year, and the average nine months. This profile is based on seven cases from the study.

Demographics

None of the parents of the women who were Self Sufficient relied on government assistance. Such was also the case for the Combiners, but not the other categories of women. The average age of the Self Sufficient woman at the time she first became a parent was 22. This was three-and-one-half years later than the Welfare Dependent group and two years later than those in Temporary Poverty. While later than the other women in the study, the time of first conception was nevertheless considerably younger than for females in the general population. Nationally, the average age for marriage is 24, which is two to six years later than when the women in the present study first conceived. The Self Sufficient category is the first group who were all married at first birth. Moreover, they had an average of only 2.3 children, the lowest of all groups. This group was comprised of European Americans in every case. What follows is the story of the Self Sufficient women.

These women, without exception, reported that they relied on medical assistance because they did not have insurance through their or their husband's employers. Today the Self Sufficient women are on average 30 years old. It has been around eight years since they first gave birth at around age 22. In over half of the cases the Self Sufficient women were presently working as were their husbands, making this the highest earnings group. The female's average net income was around $850 per month while the partners brought home an average of $1,250, or one-third more than them. In just under half (3) of the cases the Self Sufficient families owned and had paid for their homes. The following quotes from Sharon, whose case study is featured, Veronica, Mary and other women who are Self Sufficient illustrate the life experiences associated with this type of poverty in the United States.

Sharon, a European American, is 37 years old. She has three children ages seven, seventeen and twenty. She also miscarried at 18. Each child is from a different partner, to whom she was married. She has been with her present husband, Terry, for 11 years. He works as a bell boy at a sports club and she works in retail. They supplement their income by breeding dogs. Both Sharon and Terry currently receive full benefits at their places of employment. However, at the time of her previous pregnancies, neither she or her former spouse had hospitalization. Sharon's family rents the home in which they have lived for 11 years. Here is Sharon's and the other Self Sufficient women's story.

While Growing Up With My Family
Only two Self Sufficient women were raised in female headed households as teens. This is comparable to those who were in Temporary Poverty and the Combiners, but considerably fewer than the two-thirds of the Welfare Dependent and Cyclers. As with the other groups, the fathers of the Self

Sufficient women most frequently worked in upper level manual positions such as carpentry, plumbing or trucking and in high wage nonmanual service positions such as sales and teaching. Most of the mothers of the Self Sufficient women were employed; only two were full-time homemakers. Around one-half of their mothers worked in mid-wage nonmanual positions such as fast food management, health care and teaching. The others were employed in clerical and assembly line positions. One mother was on disability. The average number of sibling in their homes while growing up was 2.7. In two cases the Self Sufficient woman was an only child. None of the women reported growing up in extended families. Three Self Sufficient women rated their housing while growing up as crowded, none as overcrowded. The others rated theirs as comfortable, none as spacious. These women's sisters first gave birth at 19 years old; however, three of them were half sisters who may not have been raised in the same family except for a brief period. Two of the sisters have not yet given birth. The average age of the sisters' first births was older than the sisters of those in Temporary Poverty, but about the same as the Combiner's sisters, age 20. The Self Sufficient women's sisters are currently employed in clerical, health care and supervisory positions. Sharon, whose life was profiled at the beginning of this section, recalled the following family histories:

> Sharon's parents made her get married when she got pregnant at 18. Her mother is a nurse. Her mother has been married several times. Sharon's biological father was a drunk. Her parents have never been on government assistance.

> Veronica, on the other hand, felt her parents were not good money managers. They both own a small business in which Veronica also worked. She said her parents have gone through several inheritances and Veronica's husband has just co-signed a loan for their business.

Other Self Sufficient women reported different types of family situations. One woman who married her childhood sweetheart at age 16 and is still married to him relayed the following family history:

Her father worked in sales and her mother was a homemaker. They lived on a farm part of the time while she was growing up. During the interview she reported, "We were on government assistance once because the house burned down. There were 11 kids when I was a teen but that was because it was hers, mine and ours. A lot of them we don't have contact with today, and I'm not sure what they do for a living."

Sexual Activity

The modal ages at which the Self Sufficient women began sexual activity were 15 and 17; the mean was 16. This is comparable to the other groups. The youngest age at which the Self Sufficient women began sexual relations was 14 and the oldest, who was also the oldest in the entire sample, was 19. The most frequent place in which sexual activity occurred differed for this group. Coitus occurred most frequently in a car, followed by a house, either their own or their boyfriends, and only then, one of their parent's homes. Menstrual periods commonly began at ages twelve or thirteen. The onset of menses occurred between two to over three years prior to the initiation of sexual activity. The Self Sufficient women engaged in sexual activity between twice a week to once a year. Over half of the women, including Sharon, were sexually active with only one partner whom they eventually married. Sharon recalled:

Her parents made her get married when she got pregnant. He was 18 and had recently joined the Navy. Sharon had dropped out of school one year earlier, after the 10th grade. They are now divorced.

Another woman who was interviewed had this to say:

"As a teen you think nothing can happen to you." But it does; she got pregnant at 16 and gave birth at 17. It could have been sooner. She was not using any contraception and was having sex with multiple partners, yet did not get pregnant until two years after beginning sexual activity. Some women are just more fortunate than others.

Five of the seven women in the Self Sufficient category did not use contraception regularly. One used contraception occasionally and was the first to conceive. She used the pill about 10 percent of the time, had sex every other month, and was pregnant within four months. On the other hand, those women who never used contraception took between one to three years to get pregnant in contrast to the Welfare Dependent group, even though they engaged in sexual activity as frequently as twice a week. Most women, regardless of contraceptive use, stated that they did not really think about whether or not they would get pregnant. Two Self Sufficient women used contraception regularly. Glenda quit four months after she married in order to get pregnant without her partner's knowledge. Trudy, the other woman who used contraception regularly, became nauseated and quit taking the pill. She then switched to condoms, but was inconsistent in their use and got pregnant. Trudy recalled these events:

> She married at 16. He was her only sexual partner. They had sex once before marriage, at his apartment. They got married while she was still in high school. Alan was out of high school and had just turned 19. Three years later they had their first child. Trudy mused, "We hadn't planned to have the baby, but the condoms we were using didn't work right."

Veronica's early sexual experiences were quite different. She stated:

> "I had miscarriages at 18 and 25. It was about a year after I first began having sex. I was in college at the time of the first miscarriage and dropped out." She has yet to return to school. Veronica did not have prenatal care during the miscarried pregnancies.

Intimate Relationships

Every woman in the Self Sufficient category was married at first birth even though only two pregnancies were planned. They differ from the Temporary Poverty group in the rate of divorce. While all but one Temporary Poverty woman divorced, only two of the Self Sufficient did so, and they subsequently remarried. This is an important difference and is probably the reason that most Self Sufficient women have not experienced a dip into poverty. No one was unmarried at first birth nor was currently unmarried, creating a stark contrast to the Welfare Dependent group. Co-residing with an economically stable male partner, some self-reliant women might be more appropriately titled husband-reliant. Without husbands, women such as Veronica who was introduced earlier, would be Welfare Dependent, and may therefore feel trapped:

> Veronica works in the toy store her parents own. She clears $350 every two weeks and does not have benefits. She wants out but, "can't afford to raise three kids on my own. He makes good money." They live in his mobile home which he owned before they married. At that time, Veronica was 20 and he was 30. They live on his family's land. She has no money invested in their home even though she and Eddie have been married for 14 years. The other day she told Eddie, I don't want to *fuck* without being kissed. Since she can't *get out,* Veronica parties until 3:00 or 4:00 in the morning, and gets by on four hours sleep. Her husband, Eddie, puts the three kids to bed after picking them up from the baby sitters when he gets home from work—Veronica stays out.

Not all the women were trapped in unhappy marriages. Mary and I sat on the porch swing as she reflected on her marriage:

> She quit high school at 16 and married her former husband at 17. After four years they divorced because he beat her and was unfaithful. After living with her present husband, Jed, for 10 years, they decided to marry so the baby would have his name. She had been trying to get pregnant for 16 years. Mary and Jed just had their second child a few months ago.

Another Self Sufficient woman related the following experience:

> "We have been married for seven years. We share the household chores." Her husband gives her time alone when she needs to get away and they both make spending time alone without the kids a priority. They got married at 16 and had their first child three years later. They have two children.

Education and Employment

Of the seven Self Sufficient women, three (one of whom miscarried) had not completed high school prior to becoming pregnant. Sharon, who was featured in the opening case study, quit during her junior year, prior to her pregnancy, and has never returned. Another woman quit during pregnancy but then returned and subsequently went on to take additional training at Vo-Tech. Below are their stories:

> Sharon quit school in the 10th grade, about one year before she got pregnant, because of being bussed to a new school. That was over 20 years ago. She does not see any reason to go back to school at this time. Sharon has a good job which she loves with Bannon Fabrics with full benefits. Sharon stated, "I can always return to dog grooming if I need to."

> Trudy works as secretary for a construction company. She reported, "I couldn't finish my last year of school. There was a homebound program that brought me my schoolwork but I was just too sick to keep up." She quit one month into her pregnancy. Trudy's husband, Alan, had already graduated. She eventually got her GED and went on to Vo-Tech. Her husband's grandparents took care of the children so she could return to school. This winter, both Trudy and Alan are entering the university.

Five Self Sufficient women had completed high school (two had some college) and were working at the time they became pregnant. One of the most critical issues many women in the study faced during pregnancy was having to quit or being forced to resign from their jobs because of the strenuous nature of the work or health complications. Many women lose their jobs at this time. Should the women eventually return to work, they essentially start over in new positions, with beginning salaries. Connie's work experience follows:

> Connie got pregnant at 22. She had to quit work because of a troubled pregnancy. At that time, she qualified for Medicaid to help pay for the delivery. At the time of her second pregnancy, Connie and her husband earned too much to qualify for Medicaid. They paid cash for the child's delivery. Connie never went back to work. She stays home as a full-time caretaker for her two kids and grandmother. Connie also cared for her grandfather until he passed away recently. Connie said, "I'm happy, but I never have any time for myself."

Government and Kinship Assistance
As stated earlier, the biggest problem for the women in this group is the lack of medical coverage at their or their husband's jobs. Most, not all, were able to receive medical coverage for the deliveries of their children. The government assisted medical care typically ended shortly after pregnancy. Those women without hospitalization expressed a constant concern of how to pay the bills should one of the family get sick. Connie continued telling her life story with an example:

> When her husband's employer changed insurance companies, he and Connie were turned down for insurance because of his existing illness. They do not attempt to carry insurance themselves because of the cost for a family of four. Connie said, "If I get sick I wait to see if I get over it. For the kids, I have an uncle who is a pediatrician. He gives us a prescription if its simple (illness) or we go to a private physician and make payments." They paid cash for the last child's birth.

Dreams for the Future

Connie, the caretaker, is 30 but when I asked about her dreams she was startled, and said, "It has been so long since I thought about it, I've forgotten how to dream about things for me."

Mary and her family taught me a lot about life as we sat and talked outside in the beautiful country. I played on the swings with her oldest child as Mary rocked the baby. Mary and her husband don't make much money but they don't need much to live on. To supplement, they have a garden and cut firewood. He makes money at odd jobs because his work in the oil fields tends to be quite irregular. Mary chooses to stay home and raise the family. Mary told me, "We don't want to have the kids raised or cared for by someone else or put into day care." They bought the acreage and their stripped house for $2,500. Money is tight; last year they lived on $6,000 plus what they earned in the informal economy.

Concluding Observations

Toward the end of the fieldwork I was eating in a trendy restaurant in Oklahoma City. I was struck by the contrast between the women's lives who comprise this study and the people in the restaurant eating, drinking, and indulging, so far removed from the paucity of opportunity for the women in poverty. I sat eating my Polenta, a poor people's food in Italy eaten by those who cannot afford meat, as I watched those in the restaurant order more than they could eat, and of whatever pleased them. At the same time those in the *not so lucky* class in Italy eat Polenta and in the *not so lucky* class in Oklahoma boil neck bones or eat beans and hot dogs, and play behind darkened curtains, or in cement prisons behind security fences that only partially shield them from the outside dangers, and likewise shield them from view by those in the *lucky class.*

The life history and ethnographic observations yielded several themes that consistently ran through the stories of the women I met. These themes came through often during the interviews when I asked about their most important financial and relationship concerns, and their dreams for themselves and their children for the future.

1. The Calgon Take Me Away Syndrome: Some women felt they were stuck at home with young kids, little extra income to hire a sitter or spend and an absent or working spouse. Some of the women were in happy marriages, while others felt unfulfilled in the marriage but did not want to leave because their financial circumstances would become even worse.

2. The Welfare-Based Parenting Syndrome: A second theme I encountered in the lives of these women was that sometimes welfare takes the place of an absent parent's financial support. Some of these women had emotional support from a male partner, while others did not. All looked forward to the day when they could work and "get off welfare."

3. A Mother's Work Is Never Done Syndrome: In the majority of cases the female had the primary parenting role. Some fathers were present but many were not involved in the day to day worries of child rearing. Even when working, the female had the primary responsibility for the child care, errands, cooking, laundry, and cleaning. Often an older sibling took on child care, such errands as running to the corner grocery, or housework. Some women were more fortunate with assistance in child care and household chores than others.

4. Education is the Answer Syndrome: There was a common theme that education is the ivory tower that will make things easier, especially financially. While some of the women did not express an interest in returning to school themselves, almost without exception they wanted their children to have a better education.

5. Is This All There Is—Is There Life Out There Syndrome: Some of the females, while happy to have had their families, have postponed their dreams of careers and education in order to be the primary caretakers. They are very fulfilled in the parenting and spouse areas but feel they have achieved little in the productive or achievement related areas of life. Their female friends' lives tend to parallel their own and they, therefore, lack career–oriented role models; however, their husbands tend to have separate work and domestic spheres in their lives.

6. *I Want to Raise My Kids Myself Syndrome:* Many of the women and their husbands do not go out and leave their kids with a baby sitter. Child care is in the home by a relative or the kids accompany them. Many of the women choose not to work because they want to be responsible for rearing their own children. Each had important ideas on how their children should be raised.

7. *A Night Out Alone—Once in a Blue Moon Syndrome:* Many of the women simply do not go out without the kids or alone with their husbands. Many said they have not been out on dates or with their husbands alone since the kids were born or, if in a second marriage, never because they brought kids to it. TV is their entertainment; activities with relatives, is their support network.

8. *Can I Make It On My Own—Who Needs a Man Syndrome:* Many of the women I interviewed are very happy in their marriages. Others, however, would like to leave but have low earning power and perceive they could not support their children or would be on welfare if their husbands or they decided to divorce. They are homemakers without post-secondary education and are dependent upon their husband's higher blue collar wages for survival. On the other hand, many of the unmarried women would like to marry but are in no hurry and would rather stay single, either on welfare or at low wage jobs, than marry a man that is not going to treat them well.

NOTES

1. For all cases in the study, receiving Social Security because of a death or receiving food stamps for a period of less than six months, while technically are forms of government assistance, were not considered as such for the purposes of calculating parental socioeconomic status.

V

Statistical Analysis

Univariate Statistics: Sample Data

The sample consisted of 47 women—33 European Americans, 13 African Americans and one Native American. The Native American was not evaluated in the statistical analysis because of the limited sample. Ten African American and 28 European American women were age 18 or older (older mothers) when first giving birth. Eight of them gave birth at age 18. Among the older mothers, seven of the ten African Americans and three of the 24 European Americans were unmarried. The average age at first birth was 19.8 years for the older mothers. The average number of children was 3.3 for African American and 2.4 for European American.

Eight women (17 percent of the sample) gave birth at 17 or younger (younger mothers), four were European American and four were African American. Their average age at first birth was 16.4 overall, specifically 16 and 16.8 among African Americans and European Americans respectively. The average number of children in their families is 3.3 for African American and 3 for European American. One-half of the young mothers were unmarried. Three were African American and one was European American. Three women who were unmarried, never married, and remain welfare dependent.

Regardless of the age at first birth, 32 percent of the sample were unmarried at the time of that birth. Seven (15 percent of the sample), including three younger mothers, never married and have remained welfare dependent. All the women who remained unmarried were African American.

The currently unmarried African American women who gave birth at a young age presently received an average of $1483 in subsidized income (including housing). The currently married European American women who were young mothers received no subsidized income (see Figure 9). They earned an average net monthly income of $929, but when combined with their husband's earnings, the families' average take-home monthly income increased to $1692 (see Figures 7 and 8).

The average subsidized income for those currently unmarried who gave birth at age 18 or older was $816 among African American women and $316 among European American women. Unmarried African American and European American women who gave birth when older generally combined earned income with subsidies that averaged $804 and $749 respectively. Currently married women who gave birth at 18 or older relied primarily on earned income. The married African American women received no subsidies and the European American women received an average of $411. The married women earned a net monthly income averaging $419 (part time) and $970, for African American and European American women respectively (see Figure 7 and 8). Their respective male partners earned considerably greater—$1432 and $1215 net per month.

Reliance on government assistance varied greatly among the women in the study. The young mothers who are currently unmarried have received food stamps 36 percent of their adult lives and AFDC around the same percent of time. However, the currently married young mothers relied on stamps only 4.0 percent and AFDC 0.07 percent of their adult lives. The unmarried older mothers have relied on food stamps an average of 19 percent and AFDC an average of 15 percent of their lives. Those currently married who gave birth at age 18 or older relied on stamps 9.5 percent and AFDC 2.2 percent of their adult lives (see Figure 10).The demographic characteristics of the sample are further illustrated in Table 9.

Univariate Statistics: State Data

The State Department of Health's Pregnancy Risk Assessment Monitoring System (1992a/b, 1994) identified the following characteristics regarding women who gave birth in their teens. Statewide, 70 percent of those who gave birth at age 17 or younger relied on Medicaid for their deliveries. The trend was comparable to the findings of the present study, although the women in the sample (all except one of whom were Medicaid recipients at the time they enrolled in the study) who relied on Medicaid for the first delivery was higher—90 percent. The Department of Health and the present study also found that one-third of young mothers did not begin prenatal care in the first trimester. Four women in the present study received no prenatal care until the time of delivery or miscarriage. The primary reasons the women in the present study did not begin prenatal care included waiting to see if they would begin menstruating again, or continued to do so for the first few months, or because they were uncertain what to do about their circumstances. This concurred with the state level findings that most teens do not recognize or do not *choose* to recognize that they are pregnant in time to get first trimester care.

State data on educational attainment for teen mothers differed from the sample data. Statewide, only 50 percent of those who gave birth at age 17 or younger completed high school. In the present sample, the completion rate nearly matched the statewide rate of 90 percent. Many of the women in the study stressed the importance of GED programs, AFDC regulations and special programs for pregnant teens as reasons they were able finish high school.

At the state level, three-fourths of teen mothers were unmarried. In the present study, the marital status of young mothers differed by ethnicity. One of five European American teen mothers was unmarried; whereas, all three African American teen mothers were unmarried. At the state level (Table 3), over twice as many young European Americans were unmarried at the time of first birth compared to the present sample. It is difficult to assess the reason for the percentage differences because of the small sample size of the present sample. While the percentages differ, the marriage trends for the eight young mothers generally follow the state level data gathered by the Department of Health as shown below.

Table 3

Nonmarital Births Age 17 or Younger

	African American	European American
State	95%	65%
Sample	100%	25%

Finally, the data of the present study corroborated the findings at the state level that most births to teens were unintended. The incidence of teen contraceptive use was sporadic or nonexistent. The present study explores each of the characteristics associated with teen pregnancy in further detail in the data that follow.

Bivariate Statistics

Stage One: Time Prior to First Birth
Hypothesis One: There is a positive association between parental reliance on government assistance and a female's risk for entering and staying in poverty while adjusting for ethnicity.

Parental SES

The impact of one's environment during the teen years has important consequences for future opportunities. Some researchers suggest that nothing affects future education, occupation and income opportunities as much as our birth into a particular family (cf. Macionis 1995). Parental reliance on government assistance is an important, though not the only, indicator of a woman's family of origin's socioeconomic status. A composite measure of a high risk parental environment during adolescence was therefore developed based on the findings of previous poverty researchers (cf. Hogan and Kitagawa 1985). Six variables were used to assess a woman's degree of environmental risk during adolescence. The multiple measure was then tested for its ability to predict a female's current economic well-being. The composite measure of a high risk environment during adolescence is based on the following variables: (1) degree of parental reliance on assistance, (2) the female's perception of household living space while growing up, (3) family structure as a teen, (4) age at which the sisters first gave birth, (5) father's occupation, and/or (6) mother's occupation.

Unfortunately, only one female in the study fit all five of the criteria for a high risk environment. Even when testing the effects of the two most important variables, namely, parental reliance on government assistance (10 cases) and a sister giving birth before age 17 (9 cases), only four cases contained both variables. It was therefore decided to use only the strongest indicator, parental reliance on government assistance in the mulitvariate analysis and discuss each variable of the composite measure separately.

Variable One: Government Assistance
Thirty-seven (79 percent of the sample) of the women in the study's parents never received government assistance and 10 women (21 percent of the sample) did. Around half of those whose parents relied on government assistance (13 percent of the sample) stated they did so always or frequently; the others did so sometimes or rarely. Which parents relied on government assistance differs by the current poverty category

of the females as noted in Table 5. The statistical odds that a family of origin relied on government assistance while a woman was a teen were 3.3 for those who had their first pregnancy at age 17 or younger than for those who gave birth later. Further, there is a positive correlation of ($r = 0.46$) between parental reliance on government assistance and the amount of subsidized income a women currently receives. The correlation is statistically significant ($p = 0.001$). These findings suggest some intergenerational reliance on government assistance can be a surrogate measure of marital status because of government regulations and, therefore, may be confounded by ethnicity since a higher proportion of African Americans never married.

Variable Two: Housing Conditions
The majority of the women did not perceive their houses as crowded while growing up when they compared the number of persons to the amount of living space. Only five (11 percent) women rated their housing as overcrowded, 11 (23 percent) as crowded, 25 (53 percent) as comfortable, and six (13 percent) rated their housing as spacious.

Variable Three: Family Structure
Few of the women lived in extended families or with other relatives while growing up. Most lived in either female headed or married couple families. Nearly two-thirds were living with two parents in the home. Thirty-eight percent (18) lived with a mother and biological father, 19 percent (9) with a mother and stepfather. Only one-third of the women—38 percent (18) lived in a female headed household.

Variable Four: Age of Sister's First Pregnancy
Of those women who had older sisters, 12 (46 percent of the sample) of the siblings had a child at or before the age of 17. The median age at which the female's oldest sister first gave birth was 18, the youngest 13, and the oldest 23. The median age at which the female's second sister gave birth was slightly higher. Their ages at first birth ranged from 16 to 30, while the median age was 20.5. In those cases where a third sister was present, the age for first birth was between the ages of 16 and 28. The situation changed when a fourth sister was present. The age at which their

first birth occurred among these siblings was quite young, between 14 to 17. The early age of first birth among the latter group of women could not be evaluated statistically, however, because of the small sample size. Only one birth occurred to a fifth sister.

Variable Five: Parent's Occupation

The final measure of parental SES was the occupations of the female's parents. Each woman was asked her parents' occupation during her early teen years. Each occupation was then ranked and scored based on the type of occupation and place of employment. The difficulties associated with retrospective reporting of income make a more specific ranked scoring of the actual income associated with their occupations unreliable. It was, therefore, decided to use a more general ranking rather than risk having the females guess their parent's income while she was an adolescent.

In spite of not having the actual wage earned by her parents, the occupation type and a rough estimate of its pay scale was assessed. Each occupation was ranked into low, middle and high wage and manual or nonmanual types of labor. The occupation categories of manual and nonmanual were derived from the standard classifications used by stratification researchers, (cf. Beeghley 1989; Kerbo 1996). If the average pay for that type of employment was $5.00 or less, the wages were classified as low, wages of $8.00 or less were classified as middle, and wages above $8.00 per hour were classified as high wages (cf. Statistical Abstract of Oklahoma: 1995, Manpower Information for Affirmative Action Programs: 1990).

The mothers of the women generally were concentrated into low or high level nonmanual positions; whereas the fathers tended to be concentrated in high wage manual employment. Their occupations tended to be segregated according to gender. Women were concentrated in low wage service positions such as clerical, sales and health services. Or, less frequently they were concentrated in low wage manual positions such as cooking. On the other hand, fathers were concentrated in higher wage manual positions such as assembly line work.

A number of parents, primarily males, were working in central sector rather than peripheral markets because of employment at Tinker Air Force Base. One-third of the fathers could not be ranked because they were not present while the female was growing up. Of those who were present, three were retired or were receiving disability insurance because of health problems. Over half of the employed fathers worked upper wage manual positions. Around one-fourth were concentrated in low wage nonmanual service positions while the other one-fourth were in high wage nonmanual positions. Only two fathers were reported to be working in lower wage manual positions.

Around one-fourth of the females' mothers were homemakers who had other sources of income. Two were on disability or social security insurance. Among those employed, 38 percent were concentrated in low wage nonmanual and 11 percent in low wage manual positions. Significantly, only 6 percent of the females were in upper wage manual positions as compared to 50 percent of the males. Also, only half as many were in high wage nonmanual positions—11 percent compared to 25 percent of the males. The effect of parental reliance on government assistance on the women's chances of poverty is addressed in the multivariate analysis section.

Menses

Hypothesis Two: Females who experience earlier onset of menarche are more likely to begin sexual intercourse at an earlier age while adjusting for ethnicity.

There are strong cultural rules that guide sexual behavior in our culture, indeed in all cultures. These rules create a range of acceptable behavior that is associated with when it is appropriate to begin sexual activity. As one woman who was interviewed reported, she was about to turn 18 and was still a virgin. She wanted to have sex before her eighteenth birthday because of pressure from her friends to do so. The data of this study tend to agree with this woman's perception regarding when women begin intercourse. No one in the study reported initiating sexual activity later than age 19. A woman in our society knows the rules that guide behavior and that label us part of the 'ingroup' or 'outgroup'. Consistently, in this study, women began to engage in sexual activity between the ages of 15 to 17, almost without exception and regardless of when menarche occurred. Seventy-five percent of the women initiated sexual activity between 15 and 17. Fourteen and 18 were stretching the rules in both directions. Before turning 16, fully 39 percent of women had become sexually active. The mean age for time of first intercourse was 15.8, the median and mode was 16.

An earlier onset of menses will biologically prepare some women for intercourse sooner. Frische (1988) and others make a strong case for an earlier reproductive ability associated with industrialism because of better nutrition and a more sedentary lifestyle. One question, however, is whether there is an association between early occurrence of menses and initiation of sexual activity, or whether cultural norms associated with intercourse prevail. A Pearson's partial correlation estimate found that there was no statistically significant association between an earlier onset of menses and earlier initiation of sexual activity, while holding ethnicity constant. The correlation between the time of menses and first intercourse was 0.14 (p = 0.36), while adjusting for ethnicity; this was not statistically significant at the 0.05 level of significance; therefore, the null hypothesis could not be rejected.

The average age at which menses occurred among women in the present sample was 11.9 years; the median and mode were 12 years. This means that on average a female became sexually active four years after reaching menarche, since the average age for initiating intercourse was 16. Seventy-five percent of the women reported it was three or more years between the onset of menses and intercourse. Only 13 percent reported one year or less.

Sexual Activity

Hypothesis Three: There is a positive association between the time of first intercourse and age at time of first birth while adjusting for ethnicity.

There are three factors associated with sexual activity that can influence age of first pregnancy. First, is the frequency at which intercourse occurs. As stated in the Ethnographic Analysis section, some women unintentionally had better timing than others. The interviewees reported engaging in sexual activity between once a year to several times a week. The average was around once every two weeks. Coitus most frequently took place, 35 percent of the time, in his or her parent's home. The next most frequent places were the boyfriend's home, someone else's home—usually a relative's, or less frequently, a car. The association between frequency of intercourse and time of first pregnancy was analyzed using a partial correlation estimate. There was only a 0.08, p = 0.64 (unadjusted 0.12, p = 0.46) association between the frequency of intercourse and the age at which a female gave birth, when adjusted for ethnicity. Even when the contraceptive practice is held constant, there is only a correlation of 0.11 (p = 0.54) between frequency of sexual activity and age of first birth.

The second factor that can affect the time of first pregnancy is the age at which coitus is initiated. The earlier the initiation of sexual activity, the greater the potential risk for pregnancy to occur. The data of this study suggest that other factors also are at work. The correlation estimate of the relationship between age at first intercourse and age at first pregnancy was only 0.35 while adjusting for ethnicity. While the association was statistically significant (p = 0.02), it only explains 35 percent of the variance. The data then suggest that there is a positive association between age of first intercourse and age of first birth. Thus the null hypothesis could be rejected; however, other factors are also affecting the timing of first pregnancy.

On the average, the women consistently began to engage in sexual relations around ages 15 to 17. The most frequent time of first pregnancy was during the senior year, or around age 17. As noted in the correlation estimate, this was not necessarily associated with first coitus. The women reported that sexual relations most often took place with primarily one partner (76 percent) rather than multiple partners (24 percent) as has been noted in the literature on teen pregnancy. Moreover, in 21 percent of the cases it was with her future spouse. In 13 percent of the cases, sexual relations with her first partner resulted in pregnancy. This reported behavior differed from the literature that suggests teens engage in recreational sex with more than one partner. While the teens in the present study may have considered sex part of a recreational package, it was seldom with multiple partners (only 25 percent of the time) and one-fifth (21 percent) of the time with a partner they eventually married.

The time between first coitus and first pregnancy ranged from the first time a women engaged in sexual activity to over three years. A rather surprising finding was that in 13 percent of the cases the women got pregnant within one month of the first time she had sex. Fully 28 percent of the women were pregnant within six months; this trend is consistent with the findings of other studies of teen pregnancy. The literature suggests that there is an association between early pregnancy among these women and environment. The data in this study did not indicate a relationship between early pregnancy and other teens in the neighborhood becoming pregnant. The small sample of school age pregnancies in the study may have been a factor. The women reported no greater occurrence of teen pregnancy in their neighborhood and the others in the study. Around one-quarter of all the women reported it was very common for other teens in the neighborhood to become pregnant. Others (30 percent) said it occurred sometimes, while the others reported the occurrence as occasional or rare.

The final factor that may be associated with intercourse and first pregnancy is the consistent and correct use of contraception. Fully 59 percent of the sample reported contraceptive use as seldom or never. Only one-fourth reported using it all the time. When asked if it was being used at the time of pregnancy, only 11 percent said it was being used every time, while 62 percent said rarely or never. The others reported usage ranged somewhere in between.

The major types of contraception the women reported using were birth control pills and condoms. Each had its own associated problems. Those using pills had problems adjusting to the right brand, running out of pills, and not taking them consistently. Those using condoms reported problems using them consistently, despite good intentions. However, the major problem mentioned by the majority of women was that "they did not really think much one way or the other" about whether they would get pregnant. As a result, neither the women nor their partners, made the effort to go through the necessary channels to acquire contraception and consistently use it, even though they were aware that x can sometimes cause y.

Age, Marital Status at First Birth, and Ethnicity

Stage Two: Time of First Birth

Hypothesis Four: Females who have their first child at a younger age are more likely to enter poverty and do so for more persistent periods than females who have their first child when older, while adjusting for ethnicity and stage one variables.

Hypothesis Five: Females who are unmarried at the time of their first child are more likely to enter poverty and do so for more persistent periods than females who are married at the time of their first child, while adjusting for ethnicity and stage one variables.

Hypothesis Six: There is an interaction between age at first birth and marital status. The proportion of females who have their first child at a younger age and are unmarried at that time are at the greatest risk of entering poverty and do so for the most persistent periods after adjusting for stage one factors.

Hypothesis Seven: There is an interaction between age at first birth, marital status and ethnicity. The rates of age specific parenthood for young, unmarried African American women will be greater than for young, unmarried European American women.

On average, the women first began to parent at 19.8 years of age. The age at first birth differs by ethnicity. African American women gave birth on average at 18.6 years of age while European Americans did so at 20.2 years of age. For some of the analysis, the sample was divided into four groups: those married and unmarried females who gave birth at age 17 or younger (school age pregnancies) and those married and unmarried females who gave birth at age 18 or older. Only 17 percent of the sample gave birth at age 17 or younger; 83 percent were older. Figure 11 compares age and marital status at first birth by poverty outcomes. Half of those who had children at age 17 or younger were unmarried; whereas, only 32 percent of those who gave birth at age 18 or older were unmarried. An odds ratio was computed to estimate the risk for being unmarried if a women gives birth at a young age (17 or younger). The odds of being unmarried if giving birth at a younger versus an older age is 2.54. Three African American and five European American gave birth at age 17 or younger (young mothers). The age of first birth is lower for those who are African American, by nearly one year (16 to 16.8).

None of the young African American women were married while four of five of the European American women were married. The odds of a young African American female being unmarried at first birth were 4:1 when compared to the young European American women in the sample. When stratified across ethnicity, for all African American and European women, both young and older, the odds of being unmarried at first birth are 3.7 compared to 1.5, respectively.

These findings support the study hypothesis that predicted an association between age at first birth, marital status and ethnicity. This association, however, does not correspond with economic well–being later in life, if subsequent marital status is considered. These data also support the trends found at the state levels. The differences in marriage rates by ethnicity suggest that both variables are highly correlated. The data support hypothesis seven that predicted a positive association between marital status and ethnicity. Regardless of the age at first birth, roughly one-third (32 percent) of the women were unmarried at the time of first birth. Fifteen percent (7) of those who were unmarried at first birth, never married. These seven were African American and remained welfare dependent. Ethnicity and its interaction with marital status is discussed more fully in the Multivariate Analysis and Discussion sections.

It is difficult to generalize about the young, single moms because only four women are in this category. One young mother illustrates the impact of marriage later in life. She currently ranks at 148 percent of poverty level today because she married a high wage earner, even though she was unmarried and 16 at first birth. The other four school–age mothers were married when they first gave birth.

The relationship between marital status and ethnicity corroborates what other poverty researchers have found, namely, that there are different routes to female headship for European American and African American women. In the present study it is difficult to compare ethnic groups, especially married women of differing ethnicity, because of small sample size. There are only two currently married African American females in the sample. These two women have married partners who earn high incomes. Nevertheless, the findings do follow the state level Bureau of Census and Health Department data on marital status, income, and nonmarital pregnancy rates. Differences in marital rates at first birth are important, the present study shows that young, nonmarried women at first birth fare no worse economically than young, married women who later divorce.

In 70 percent of the cases the woman's partner was working at the time of the first pregnancy. In 28 percent of the cases the partner was not working. When correlated with ethnicity, it was found that European American partners of young mothers were working 75 percent of the time but among African American partners, only 20 percent were reported as working. These data were expected because of the differences in employment by ethnicity among men in their teens and 20s. (The implications are discussed more fully in the next chapter.) The differences in marriage rates also correspond with employment data. Marriage was not a rational choice for those young couples who were not economically stable. At the time of the second child, up to 75 percent of the partners were working. Whereas, among the women, 37 percent were working when pregnant with their second child. Of those who were working, several reported having to quit because of health complications during pregnancy or because of the strenuous nature of the work.

The relationship between age and marital status at first birth and poverty is a complex one. For example, there are some differences in current reliance on subsidized income and current net usable income between the young, married moms as compared to older, married moms (Figures 8, 11). In addition, there are differences simply based on marital status at first birth regardless of whether the women was a young or an older mom. For example, among the younger women who were married at first birth, the current percent of poverty level is on average 72 percent;. whereas for those who had their first child later and were married, it averages 82 percent, a 10 percent improvement (see Figure 13). Age at first birth is inversely associated ($r = -0.24$) with the proportion of time a female is on AFDC as an adult, but is not statistically significant ($p = 0.10$) at a 0.05 level of significance (see Table 6). AFDC is not the best measure of poverty status because it fluctuates with the number of children and it interacts with marital status.

Interestingly, age at first birth is negatively associated with the current amount of combined subsidized and earned income (-0.29), when adjusted for stage one variables of parental reliance on government assistance and ethnicity; martial status at first birth showed no association whatsoever to current percent of poverty level ($r = 0.08$, $p = 0.6$). The correlation of poverty and age at first birth is confusing. She may have been poorer initially, but later in life a woman's poverty situation is more influenced by her current marital status than her age and marital status at first birth. The average income for the young mothers who are currently married was only 13 percent less than the older moms who likewise are currently married. Thus, the trends were not as expected in the research hypotheses. The women who gave birth at an earlier age and were unmarried may have been poorer at the time. However, if they married later in life and remained so, whether they had a child young and whether they were married at the time made no difference in their current poverty status. It is important to remember that the comparison is made with other non-degreed women who are also poor by comparison to the general population.

Length of time on AFDC is not the best measure of poverty because, in order to qualify, a female must be separated or unmarried. However, many of the women who were married at first birth, subsequently divorced, and some in turn, remarried. Thus, it provides an interesting commentary on their life histories. Young mothers who were married at first birth, have been on AFDC an average of 11 months of their adult lives. Interestingly, two of the five young mothers who were married at first birth have never been on AFDC. Those whose teen marriages did not last, did not gain an advantage over those who waited until later to marry, but then divorced. The young moms who were single, but married later, were on AFDC an average of only 1.5 percent longer than their married counterparts. The group one would expect to have the greatest advantage were those who delayed child bearing and were also married at the time of delivery. Interestingly, when current marital status was not taken into account, these moms had a longer period of average time on AFDC, 13.9 percent of their lives. Once again, it does not seem to matter what the circumstances were when first beginning to parent; if young and single, the combined earned and subsidized income later in life is only 12 percent less than those who were married and older. This is in part because government assistance helps to alleviate the poverty that a non-married female might experience. These data are displayed in Figures 7, 8, and Table 11.

An examination of current subsidized (not including earned) income does show a correlation with age and marital status (Table 9). Those who married young and were not married have significantly higher proportions of their current income from federal subsidies. Figures 8 through 13 below show that there is an association between age and marital status at first birth and current reliance on subsidized income versus earned income. As can be seen in Figure 9 there is a positive relationship between a female's ethnicity and marital status at first birth. Ethnicity is highly correlated with total subsidized income (r = 0.54, p = 0 .0001). There is a 0.54 correlation between current subsidized income and being African American. Age at first birth (r =.15) is not associated but martial status at first birth is. Current subsidized income is lower for women who were married at first birth (-0.47, p = 0.0009). Both of these correlations are being influenced by a woman's former and current marital statuses, however, because subsidized income is generally only available to females who are unmarried. Therefore, the interaction of age, marriage and ethnicity changes when her current combined earned and subsidized income, rather than subsidized income alone, is considered (see Figures 11 and 12). This makes sense because government assistance levels raise some women to comparable economic levels with many of the working, low wage-earning poor. These effects are illustrated in the figures at the end of the chapter.

Stage Three: Time Subsequent to First Birth

Educational Attainment
Hypothesis Eight: There is an interaction between age at time of first birth and total number of children and a female's educational attainment level.

Hypothesis Nine: There is an association between subsequent educational attainment leading to increased earning power and effect on remaining or exiting poverty.

Of debate in the literature is the effect of early pregnancy on a female's subsequent educational attainment (e.g. Furstenburg 1991; Upchurch and McCarthy 1992). Even with early pregnancy, today there are enormous cultural pressures on women to complete high school eventually, even if they drop out with their first child. In the present study, all but three women who left school at or before pregnancy returned eventually. They typically expressed how proud they were of achieving their high school diploma regardless of whether they were currently working outside the home. Many of their comments were presented in the Ethnographic profile section.

When evaluating the effects of education, it is important to keep in mind that none of the women have as yet completed more than an Associate of Arts degree. Correlation estimates were run in several ways. An unadjusted correlation coefficient estimated the effect of a woman's age at first birth on current educational attainment and found no association ($r = 0.003$, $p = 0.9$). A second unadjusted correlation estimate measured the relationship between a female's current educational level and current combined subsidized and earned income and no association was found ($r = 0.09$, $p = 0.5$). However, there was a small positive association ($r = 0.25$) between current earned income (not considering subsidized income) and education, when adjusted for the biggest influence, current marital status. It tends toward, but it is not statistically significant at point 0.05 level of significance ($p = 0.10$). Next, the effect of a woman's current educational level was measured in relation to useable income (combined income minus housing and child care) as a percent of poverty level. Current marital status had little effect. When controlling for current martial status, the amount of variance in the poverty level that can be explained through education changes little ($r = 0.24$, $p = 0.10$). A final correlation estimated the effect of the total number of children in relation to current educational attainment. Again, there was a moderate association, although it was not statistically significant with an n of 46. Education was inversely related to the number of children ($r = -0.25$, $p = 0.09$).

Not all the women were in school when they first gave birth. Around one-half had been out for one or more years. Of those not in school, 25 percent were working at least part time when they became pregnant. Around half (13 percent of the total sample) of those who were working continued to do so until the child was born. Nine attempted to work afterwards but quit within one year because of the difficulty of working and raising a family. The majority of the employed women quit while pregnant. Only four women continued to work uninterrupted both during pregnancy and after the child was born. The data on work and pregnancy suggest that for women in positions of manual or low wage service employment in which unpaid pregnancy leave is unaffordable, pregnancy means the end of the job and time invested in that employment position. The reasons women quit during pregnancy varied. Eleven percent quit because of health reasons such as bleeding and swelling. Others had to resign because their physicians ordered them to do so for health complications. Several women were forced out because they could no longer lift or otherwise do what was required at work after becoming pregnant. Only one woman received pregnancy leave.

Of 47 women, 18 percent had already left school but had not graduated when they first became pregnant. Eleven women (nearly 25 percent of the sample) were in school at the time they conceived. However, half (11 percent of the sample) were seniors and graduated between the time of conception and delivery. Seven (17 percent of the sample) were also in school at the time of their second child. Some of those who became pregnant while still in school, were able to remain in school during the pregnancy because of the assistance of special educational programs, but quit after delivery. Half of the women who remained in school (11 percent of the sample) were enrolled in special programs for pregnant teens during the school year of their pregnancy. They reported such programs as important factors in enabling them to continue in school. Unfortunately, few programs provide for young mothers' special needs once the child is born; the new mothers must return to regular school and try and juggle motherhood and school.

Of those who dropped out of school, most women eventually returned, usually securing a GED. Often, after completing high school, they acquired additional training. When interviewed, women cited AFDC assistance and Pell grants as the primary reasons they were able to return to school. A third reason cited was kinship support in the form of child care assistance.

Seventeen percent of those who were in school at the time of the first pregnancy quit, but later completed high school. This suggests the importance of GED programs which enabled many of these women to complete their education. Those who quit, at or before their first pregnancy, faced tremendous societal pressure to complete high school. The importance of GED programs is clearly evidenced by this study. Nearly one-half of those having only a high school education completed the degree through GED a program. The finding on education illustrates the tremendous social pressure on individuals to complete high school. Only two women in the study have not yet completed high school. As noted above, a major reason many were able to complete school while pregnant is because they became pregnant during their senior year and graduated before delivery or were able to enroll in special programs available to pregnant teens, especially the homebound program.

By an average of ten years later, at the time of the present interview, 38 percent of the women had received some advanced training beyond high school. Four women, or 9 percent of the sample, had completed a Vo-Tech certificate or an Associate's degree; four others were in the process of doing so. Another 38 percent had completed high school, although nearly half (42 percent) had acquired a GED rather than returning to regular school.

A major reason for the high proportion of women who went beyond a high school education is the federal requirements associated with AFDC. When asked if AFDC had required her to return to school, 22 percent of the women said yes. None of the women, however, have completed beyond an Associates degree even with these government assistance regulations. Importantly, of those who received some advanced training, none reported being employed in areas in which they received training. This may explain the lack of association between education and income. The women cited a variety of reasons for not completing the training or, among those who did, not finding employment in a related field. Some reasons cited were marriage and lack of practical experience. Several of the women were currently in school; the advantage accrued by their training could, therefore, not as yet be assessed. The lack of impact of education on income is addressed more fully in the next chapter.

Marital Status after First Birth

Hypothesis Ten: There is an association between subsequent changes in marital status, either a divorce or a marriage, and a female's risk of entering, remaining in or exiting poverty.

As noted earlier, there are different routes to female headship; some women never marry while others do so, but subsequently divorce. Perhaps one of the most important findings of the present research is the effect of divorce for women. Whether a women has never married, or was married but is now divorced, these different routes to female headship are of minimal consequence with regard to her present amount of earned and usable income or her percent of poverty level.

As will be remembered, the usable income variable includes both the net earned and subsidized income and deducts the house payment and/or house subsidy; whereas, the percent of poverty variable considers these deductions and also takes into account the number of persons in the family. The usable income is then converted to a percent of the current poverty level for the number in the family. This is an important consideration because it controls for the proportionate rise in subsidized income as family size increases. Were this not taken into account, a person having a subsidy of $1,100 may appear better off until the six children in her family are factored into the equation.

The findings comparing never married females to divorced females is as follows. The percent of poverty differed only slightly between those who married, but divorced and those who never married. Divorced females were at 69 percent of poverty level and never married females were at 62.5 percent when compared to married women who were arbitrarily set at 100 percent. However, the divorced women were considerably poorer if household level earned and subsidized income are measured without regard to family size. This is because the divorced women in the sample have fewer children. Therefore, when income was not adjusted for household size, the never married (predominantly African American) have 10 percent greater usable income than divorced women (predominantly European American). The never married women have an unadjusted (to family size) usable income rate of 59.5 percent compared to only 46.5 percent for divorced females in relation to every one dollar of income for married females.

The next question of interest was whether differences in a woman's current economic well-being occurred when the age at first birth was added to the equation. Among those who gave birth at 17 or younger, and never married or divorced, their respective adjusted (to married women) usable incomes were 71¢ and 46¢ in relation to those who had their babies young but were currently married. The young moms currently with a male marriage partner were considerably better off than those who never married or married, but then divorced. When household size was considered, the corresponding adjusted percent of poverty level improves, but also reverses, to 61 percent for never married and 80 percent for those who divorced.

These trends again reflect differences in family size and corresponding increases in subsidized income based on the number in household. Those divorced women who gave birth young are now considerably better off. This holds constant whether the women was married at first birth or not. However, the women differed in their "source" of usable income. The source of usable income for the young, never married moms was subsidized rather than earned income. None of the never married, school-age mothers had earned income; all were on government assistance. The young mothers who were unmarried at first birth, never married. The number of cases who gave birth at a young age (four married and four unmarried) is quite small so it is difficult to generalize. Earned versus subsidized income is compared in Figures at the end of the chapter.

Among those who had their children at age 18 or older, the never married and divorced women's adjusted usable income did not differ. It was 48¢ and 47¢ of those currently married. When the number in the family was taken into account, their corresponding adjusted percent of poverty level still differed only minimally; it was 63 percent and 59 percent of the married women's. Those who relied on government assistance or female-based wages were 20-50 percent worse off than those who relied on husbands. Their average net earned family income differed in accord with differences in wages by gender and the work disincentives associated with federal assistance. The never married actually fared a bit better than the divorced. They earned 44¢ compared to 40¢ for every dollar a married female earned with her husband. Figure 15 and Table 10 compare all male to female earnings.

Some interesting differences begin to emerge, however, when one compares combined earned and subsidized income without considering other expenses. In this equation, total earned and subsidized income included housing vouchers and an estimation for HUD housing and regular house payments. For the purposes of this analysis, housing subsidies were considered cash. Among those who had their first child at 17 or younger, the never married and divorced women's adjusted total earned and subsidized income was much higher; their combined earned and subsidized income averaged 77¢ (standardized to married females). The nonmarried women had an average family of five. Divorced women fared much poorer. Their combined earned and subsidized income was only 49¢ compared to those currently married. These women had an average family of two, but the sample size included only two cases. Those never married who had their first child at 18 or older had an adjusted earned and subsidized income of 73¢. These women had an average family of five which is comparable to the young moms who never married. For those older moms who divorced, the combined earned and subsidized income was only 57¢. However, they had fewer in the family—an average of 3.5 persons. The combined income before housing and child care expenses are deducted, once again shows the never married to be considerably better off than the divorced, until their larger family size is considered.

There are several possible explanations for these differences in income and family size. First, the housing subsidies provided to many nonmarried women tend to be inflated because landlords sometimes overcharge the government for housing. Second, some subsidies are not actual cash the women can spend; rather they are in the form of a voucher. Third, those women who never married have more children than the divorced and married women. Thus, their subsidized income goes up proportionate to the number of children; whereas earned income does not. These factors explain the statistically significant associations of subsidized income and total number of children with ethnicity. For these reasons, the percent of poverty rather than income is a more realistic indicator of the women's current well-being. It controls for housing and the number in the family.

The net benefit to those who marry and then divorce is only 7.5¢ per dollar of usable income (when married is standardized to $1.00) when adjusted for the number in the family. How can the lack of accrued advantage to women who were married for part of their lives be explained? First, no woman received a college degree during the period of marriage. Nor did any advanced training she received result in employment in a specialized field with income advantages. Second, none of the women acquired an interest in a home equity while married, even when the homes were paid for. Perhaps most interesting, however, is the third point. Only three of the women received child support from their former spouses, even when it was awarded by the state. This last circumstance warrants further discussion.

Our cultural rules regarding fatherhood are undergoing modification. Biological fathers are becoming less invested in their own children and more emotionally and financially invested in their stepchildren. In their biological family, they increasingly have minimal or non-existent custodial rights and obligations. They, in turn, transfer these roles, once reserved for biological fathers to their stepchildren in newly-created families. The result is that the divorced custodial partners, if not remarried or consistently receiving child support, are poorer after divorce than those of the newly-created step family.

Kinship Assistance

Hypothesis Eleven: Females who have kinship support as defined as child care, financial or shelter will be more likely to move above the poverty level.

Kinship support most often occurred in three areas. One area was child care—wherein one or more relatives watched the children while the female worked or attended school. The second area was housing, usually in the form of a family home or provisions on family land. The final area of support was errands or some form of transportation assistance. The grandparents were as likely to provide a mutual aid network as were the parents. Likewise, the assistance was just as likely to come from in-laws. The network often included support from brothers' wives and sisters. Evidence of a viable kinship network often came in the form of phone calls during the interviews. Some calls were from siblings, mothers and cousins calling to coordinate day care. In addition, nieces and nephews could often be seen playing with the women's children during interviews.

Parents and grandparents tended to help in many ways. A major area of assistance was housing, either temporarily in their homes or other housing such as a trailer on family land. This occurred when the daughter/granddaughter could not afford a separate home or when the female separated or divorced. Kinship support in the form of housing was the biggest advantage to the women. Four women (8.5 percent of the sample) who resided independently had such assistance, often living in homes owned by relatives. Another four women (8.5 percent of the sample) resided, at no cost, in homes with relatives, or occasionally, shared expenses.

Child care was the second advantage accrued through kinship support. Twelve of the employed women reported no expense for child care. Care was either provided by relatives or fully subsidized by government assistance. Others paid a relative for child care, but at a much reduced rate compared to normal day care costs.

The final form of kinship support was the exchange of errands and in recreational activities. An important part of the kinship network was the function of family members as friends. When asked about friendship activities such as shopping, eating out or entertainment, the women frequently responded that their circle of relatives were their friends. In this way, the kinship network also served as a recreation network. Leisure activities such as swimming were with various segments of the extended kinship network. Shopping, bingo or other activities also were undertaken by some women with family members, instead of friends. Rarely did any recreation or errands occur without the children accompanying them. Moreover, couples seldom pursued entertainment together, without the children present.

The kinship support system was often a reciprocal mutual aid network, as women sometimes cared for ailing grandparents, or nieces, nephews, and cousins. Usually, however, women in the study most frequently received the greatest advantage. Often the women were not totally reliant on their parents and/or grandparents. Usually, but not always, kinship assistance was provided without costs to the women's self-esteem or encroaching on their parenting roles. Parents and grandparents also tended to do quite a lot for the female's children in the way of toys, clothes, and little 'extras.' Biological fathers who were not obligated to provide child support also provided such extras in some women's lives. The support system was one of both emotional and financial advantages, but one not without potential costs of privacy and independence.

Current Poverty Status

Occupational Segregation by Gender

Abell and Lyon (1979) make the important distinction between two types of socioeconomic status—income and occupational prestige. The women in this study and their mothers were generally employed in positions associated with greater social prestige but were lagging behind their male partners in income. While it may not be very socially desirable to be a wood or assembly worker, it pays far better than retail sales or a teacher's aide. The discrimination is not necessarily directed towards the female, per se, but the occupational positions in which she is typically employed. Because of a woman's education and job choices, she is locked into occupations that pay 30 to 50 percent less than males. Three males in the study who occupied similar nonmanual service sector and low wage manual positions received comparably low wages. Nevertheless, more high wage opportunities are available to non-college educated men, although the positions do not confer great social prestige according to the prevailing cultural norms.

Income Differences by Race, Gender and Marriage
Nationally females earn 72¢ for every dollar a male earns. In Oklahoma, the income disparity is greater. According to the 1990 census data, women in Oklahoma generally earned on an average of 57¢ less than men, for every dollar of wages. The earnings of women in the present study generally corresponded to those statewide. On average they earned 52¢ for every $1.00 a male earned, keeping in mind that these are men without college degrees (Figure 15). The males in the study had wages that were between $1.37 to $2.13 more per hour than the female's hourly wages (Table 10).

A second way of comparing income is between ethnic groups. According to the 1990 census data, the average African American female earned 80¢ for every $1.00 the average European American female earned. However, when compared to every $1.00 a European American male earned, there was only 9¢ difference in income between European American and African American females (Figure 14). Economic discrimination by ethnicity exists, but the greatest economic discrimination is gender based.

A third income comparison can be made between married and unmarried females. In the present study married females earned an average net monthly income of $961. African American versus European American married females could not be compared separately because there were only two African American married females in the study; only one worked and she was part-time. Interestingly, unmarried females in the study earned less regardless of their ethnicity. Unmarried European American females netted an average of only $773 and corresponding African American females only $638. When these wages were standardized and converted to dollars per hour, for every $1.00 a married female earned, an unmarried European American female earned 80¢, and an unmarried African American female earned 66¢. When standardized to unmarried European American, African American unmarried females earned 82¢ for $1.00 earned by her European American counterpart. The differences in earnings by gender and ethnicity in the sample were compared to statewide data in Figures 4 and 5. More discussion of the differences in income is addressed in the next chapter.

Multivariate Analysis

Operational Definition of Variables

The four dependent variables were various approaches to measuring a woman's current economic well-being. The first method combined all earned income and all subsidies, including house subsidies. The "total income" variable approach should provide the best picture of a woman's net cash and subsidy income in dollars, before expenses. Next, this dollar amount (combined subsidized and earned income) was converted to an interval level percent of poverty level, which then took into account and adjusted for a female's household size.

The third dependent variable subtracted all housing costs, both subsidized and payments and also subtracted all child care costs. This "usable income" variable calculated a woman's net usable income in actual dollars in the regression equation. This variable controlled for potential confounding from inflated subsidized housing payments which, as discussed earlier, were not actual cash the female could use at her discretion.

The final dependent variable modeled in the regression equation was calculated the same as the "usable income" variable. Rather than an interval measurement in dollars, however, it also converted the dollar amount to an interval level percent of poverty and, thereby, controlled for family size. This measurement of usable income was a percent of poverty variable based on the 1995 poverty level for the female, her spouse (where applicable) and actual number of dependents in the family. It measured how well off the woman was in terms of the 1995 government calculation of the poverty level for her corresponding family size.

Stages in the Regression Model

Each of the measurements of "combined subsidized and earned" and "usable income" was regressed on the hypothesized independent variables. The effects of each independent variable were measured cumulatively (Table 7) and separately (Table 8). The first stage in the regression analysis tested the effects of risk factors associated with the adolescent period in the life cycle, or what is referred to as the "Time Before First Birth." The major hypothesis tested in the regression equation at this stage was parental economic status. This was measured by estimating the degree of parental reliance on government assistance. It was originally intended to use a composite measure to evaluate the woman's environment as a teen; as discussed earlier, however, only one female met all five characteristics. Therefore, only the greatest potential predictor was entered into the regression model, that of parental reliance on government assistance.

Stage two tested the effects of risk factors associated with time two in the life cycle, referred to as the "Time of First Birth." At this stage the major hypotheses tested were the relationship between age and marital status at time of first birth and current poverty status.

Stage three tested the effects of marriage and divorce later in life as risk factors for entering and remaining in poverty. This stage was referred to as the "Stage Subsequent to First Birth." At this stage one major hypothesis was tested: the effect of current marital status on poverty status. Each of the four major hypotheses was tested according to the appropriate stage in the life cycle (Full Model). Each variable was also tested separately, and only one variable—current marital status, was significant (Trimmed Model). Once the effect of current marital status was accounted for, the other three variables: parental SES, age at first birth, and marital status at first birth, explained little of the variance in current economic well–being. The regression equations showing the effects of the four major hypothesis on the dependent variables are shown in Tables 7 (Full Model) and 8 (Trimmed Model).

Findings of the Regression Model

The regression analyses presented unexpected results. It was originally predicted that age at first birth would have the greatest effect on income and poverty status. The multivariate analyses showed that age and marital status at first birth had little consequences on poverty status, if a woman married later in life. Of the four major hypotheses in this study, only one null hypothesis could be rejected with an alpha of 0.05: the effect of current marital status on poverty status. The regression equation showed a positive association ($p = 0.001$) between changes in marital status subsequent to a female's first child and her current economic well–being. For example, in the full model, a married woman's total usable family income was $699.79 more, on average, per month, than the income of a nonmarried women; the standardized regression coefficient was 0.589. This translates to 32.8 percent higher on the poverty level scale, with a standardized regression coefficient of 0.439. The effects of the other major hypotheses paled in importance to the effect of a woman's current marital status. These effects remained when current age and educational level were controlled for in the model. Over ten different variables were added; none added significantly to the relatively large contribution (e.g. adjusted $r = 0.32$ for total usable family income) of current marital status. The implications of the regression analysis are discussed in the next chapter.

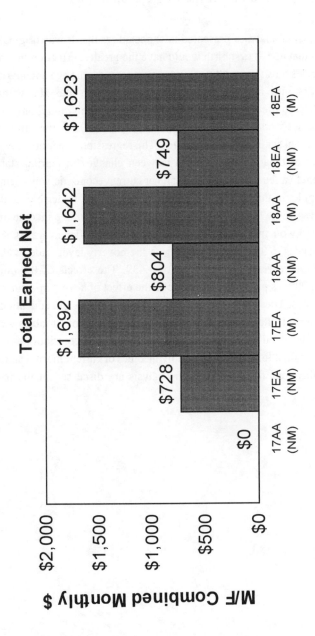

Figure 7

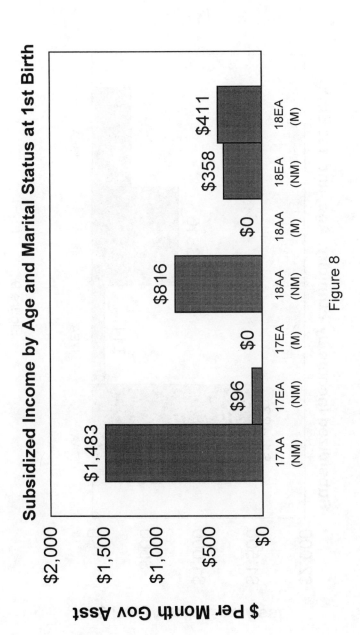

Figure 8

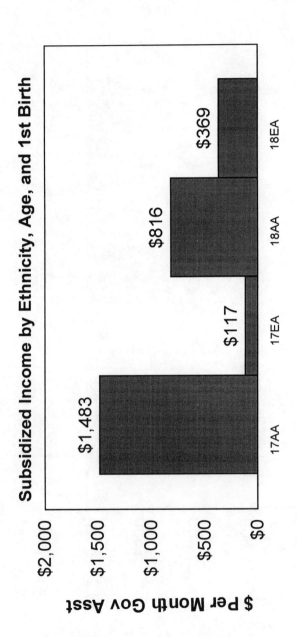

Figure 9

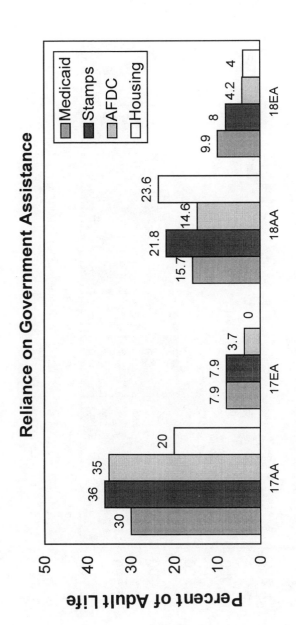

Figure 10

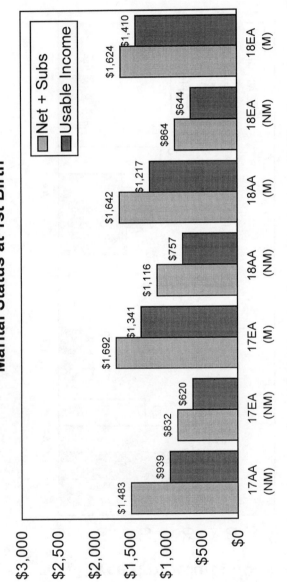

Figure 11

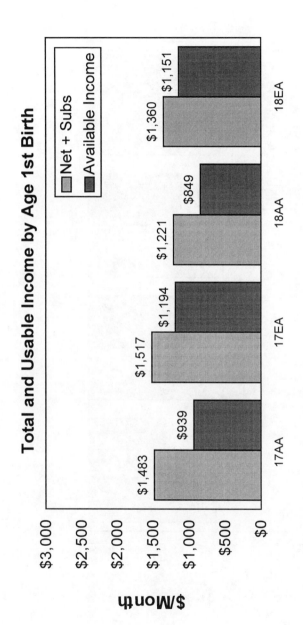

Figure 12

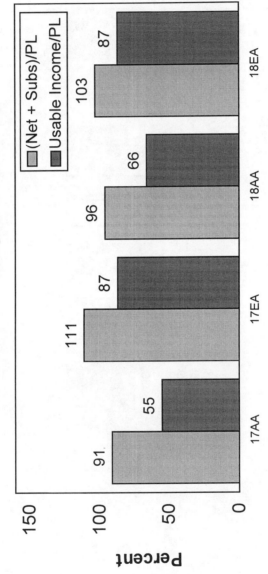

Figure 13

Table 2 Averages of Major Variables by Poverty Type

*VARIABLES BY POVERTY TYPE	WP	CYC	COM	TP	SS
Age at first birth	18.5	20.75	19	20	22
# in family	4.4	3.9	5	4	4
Potential Appropriation	705	653	671	605	610
Female Net - Approp $/m	4	48	46	251	149
Female Net - Approp $/h	0	0	0	1	1
Other Income	0	68	0	87	23
Female Net Income	92	453	304	751	495
Male Net Income	0	193	901	845	1186
Total Earned Gross(TEG)	108	740	1386	1831	2014
Total Earned Net (TEN)	92	645	1205	1597	1681
AFDC	335	38	0	0	0
Stamps	344	180	64	17	0
Housing (HS)	334	91	38	0	0
Total Subs Income (TSI)	1014	363	103	17	0
TEN + Subs	1106	1008	1308	1614	1681
Child Care Costs (CC)	0	10	10	21	50
TEN + Subs - HP	1094	823	1103	1368	1508
TEN + Subs - HS - HP	760	733	1065	1368	1508
TEN + Subs - HS - HP - CC	760	723	1056	1347	1458
TEG + Subs - HS	788	1012	1450	1848	2014
Poverty Level (PL)	1343	1236	1378	1243	1324
(TEG + Subs)/PL	55	83	106	142	152
(TEN + Subs)/PL	78	82	96	124	127
(TEN + Subs - HS)/PL	54	74	92	124	127
(TEN + Subs - HP)/PL	77	67	80	105	114
(TEN + Subs - HS - HP - CC)/PL	53	59	76	103	110
Medicaid - # of times	1.75	2.25	2	1	1
Medicaid - %	26	14	10	10	3
Stamps - # of times	38	2.13	2	1	0
Stamps - %	30	16	12	8	0
AFDC - # of times	2	1.875	0	1	0
AFDC - %	29	11	3	5	0
Housing - %	20	20	5	2	0

* See Appendix A for a description of each variable

Table 4   Demographics by Age at First Birth, Current Marital Status
and Ethnicity

*VARIABLES	Young N/M*	Young M**	Older N/M	Older N/M	Older M	Older M
Ethnicity	AA	EA	AA	EA	AA	EA
Current Age	26.5	31.5	28.6	29.3	34.2	30.2
Age at first birth	16	16.8	19.4	21	18.5	20.7
# in Family	4.3	5	3.8	3.1	5.5	4.6
Fe Net Inc-Potential GA/hr.	$0.00	$1.28	$1.36	$0.96	$1.66	$1.73
Female Net Income/mth	$0.00	$929	$804	$749	$419	$970
Male Net Income/mth	$0.00	$1,227	$0.00	$0.00	$1,432	$1.22
Subsidized Income/mth	$1,483	$0.00	$816	$358	$0.00	$411
Total Income	$1,483	$1,692	$1,116	$864	$1,642	$1,624
Usable Income	$939	$1,341	$757	$644	$1,017	$1,410
Total Income/Poverty	91%	115%	94%	84%	106%	117%
Usable Income/Poverty	55%	91%	63%	64%	79%	101%
% of Life on Medicaid	30.3%	5.3%	17.8%	15.9%	17.5%	8.1%
% of Life on Stamps	36.2%	4.0%	24.0%	14.2%	14.1%	6.3%
% of Life on AFDC	35.4%	0.7%	17.8%	11.0%	2.5%	1.9%
% of Life on Housing	19.5%	0.0%	29.5%	10.4%	0.0%	1.1%

*No Young African Americans are currently married
**No Young European Americans are currently unmarried
***See Appendix A for a description of each variable

Table 5 Parental Reliance on Government Assistance

Poverty Category	Number	Percent
Group one (Welfare Dependents)	5	62%
Group two (Cyclers)	3	38%
Group three (Combiners)	0	0%
Group four (Temporary Poverty)	2	18%
Group five (Self Sufficient)	0	0%
Total on Government Assistance	10	21%

N=47

Table 6 Averages for Variables By Ethnicity, Age, and Marital Status at 1st Birth

*VARIABLE	17AA(NM)	17EA(M)	18AA(NM)	18AA(M)	18EA(NM)	18EA(M)
Ethnicity	17AA	17EA	18AA	18AA	18EA	18EA
Age at First Birth	16.0	16.8	19.4	18.5	21.0	20.7
# in family	4.3	5	3.8	5.5	3.1	4.6
Female Net - Potential GA	0.0	1.28	1.36	-1.66	0.96	1.73
Female Income: Net	0.0	929	804	419	749	970
Male Income: Net	0.0	1227	0.0	1432	0.0	1215
Total Earned Net (TEN)	0.0	1692	804	1642	749	1623
Total Subs Income (TSI)	1483	0.0	816	0.0	358	411
TEN + Subs	1483	1692	1116	1642	864	1624
TEN + Subs - HS - HP - CC	939	1341	757	1217	644	1410
(TEN + Subs) as % of Poverty	91	115	94	106	84	117
Usable Income as % of Poverty	55	91	63	79	64	101
Age/Month	318	378	344	411	352	362
Medicaid %	30.3	5.3	17.8	7.5	15.9	8.1
Stamps %	36.2	4.0	24.0	13.1	14.2	6.3
AFDC %	35.4	0.7	17.8	2.5	11.0	1.9
Housing %	19.5	0.0	29.5	0.0	10.4	1.1
SSI %	0.0	0.0	0.0	0.0	0.0	0.4

*See Appendix A for a description of each variable

Table 7. Regression Coefficients of the Independent Determinates of Poverty: Full Model

Independ. Variables	Model One Usable Income				Model Two Usable Poverty Level				Model Three Combined Income				Model Four Combined Poverty Level			
	b	S.E.	stb	p	b	S.E.	stb	p	b	S.E.	stb	p	b	S.E.	stb	p
Parental SES	-68.87	-197.30	-0.48	0.26	-15.26	13.17	-1.73	0.23	-36.79	211.73	-0.02	0.86	-16.73	14.25	-0.17	0.24
MS 1st birth	-26.45	-211.60	-0.02	0.90	1.67	14.12	0.02	0.92	-112.54	233.55	-0.08	0.61	-8.89	15.04	-0.10	0.55
Age 1st birth	-32.38	-28.49	-0.02	0.26	-1.24	1.93	-0.10	0.51	-51.97	30.79	-0.23	0.09	-2.44	2.07	-0.17	0.24
Current MS	699.79	-198.36	0.59	0.001	32.8	113.24	0.44	0.01	699.08	200.53	0.56	0.0001	31.28	13.83	0.40	0.02
R²	0.37				0.29				0.33				0.22			
R² adj	0.31				0.23				0.27				0.14			
N	46				46				46				46			

Model One: Usable Income in Dollars
Model Two: Usable Income as a Percent of Poverty
Model Three:　Combined Net Earned and Subsidized Income in Dollars
Model Four:　Combined Net Earned and Subsidized Income as a Percent of Poverty

Table 8 Regression Coefficients of the Independent Determinates of Poverty: Trimmed Model

Independent Variables	Model One Usable Income				Model Two Usable Poverty Level				Model Three Combined Income				Model Four Combined Poverty Level			
	b	S.E.	stb	p value	b	S.E.	stb	p value	b	S.E.	stb	p value	b	S.E.	stb	p value
Current Marital Status	698	145	588	0.0001*	39	9.66	0.56	0.0002*	652	163	516	0.0002*	31	10.8	0.40	0.006*
R^2	0.35				0.27				0.27				0.16			
R^2 adj	0.33				0.25				0.25				0.14			
N	46				46				46				46			

*P<.05

Model One: Usable Income in Dollars
Model Two: Usable Income as a Percent of Poverty
Model Three: Combined Net Earned and Subsidized Income in Dollars
Model Four: Combined Net Earned and Subsidized Income as a Percent of Poverty

VI
Discussion

Limitations of the Study

Confounding and Interaction

A major question was whether the associations between current marital status and economic well-being, as estimated by the regression analysis, were confounded. Two potential areas of confounding were examined in the present study: ethnicity and male earned income. The dependent variables, current economic well-being and percent of poverty, were highly correlated with ethnicity in the model. It was found that ethnicity alone accounted for 10 percent of the variance in a woman's current economic well-being, as defined in the present study.

The important question, however, was what is actually being measured. In this sample, ethnicity was highly correlated with marital status and marital status was highly correlated with economic well-being. The key was not that the women were African American, but that African American women in this sample were more likely to be unmarried. This trend mirrors state and national data. When marital status was held constant, ethnicity explained only 10 percent of the variance in poverty status. The odds of being unmarried for African American were 7:2 compared to European American. Only two of the African American women (16 percent of the African American sample), compared to 14 (48 percent) of the European American women, were married at the time of this study. What was being measured, therefore, was the interaction between marital status and ethnicity, rather than ethnicity itself.

The second area of potential confounding was the effect of marital status. The question of interest was whether economic well-being was confounded by male earned income, and the presence of dual earners in the household. It was important to see whether the degree of variation in economic well-being was a result of income differentials between male and female earners. To explore these potential confounders, the effects of three additional independent variables were tested: male net earned income, female net earned income, and the combined earned income of dual earner couples.

Each of these variables was entered into a regression equation (Table 9) to determine its relative contribution to the earnings and subsidies that make up the usable income variable. When gender differences were calculated as a component of current economic well-being (usable income), female earnings accounted for only 14 percent of the variance in usable income; whereas male earnings accounted for 57 percent of the differences in usable income. Taken together, male and female earnings explained 75 percent of the differences found. The other 25 percent of usable income could be attributed to government subsidies and potential estimation error in the study. The role of dual earner versus single was investigated next. Eleven couples (23 percent of the sample) were dual earners. As would be expected, if both members of a couple worked, regardless of the income, it accounted for 42 percent of the variance in economic well-being.

The next step was to explore the contribution of females to the dual earner equation. This was done by combining the potential contribution of female earners with dual earners. The equation changed little. The amount of variance contributed by the female income was minimal. The R^2 for dual jobs and female earned income accounted for only 41 percent of the variance. (Dual alone without consideration for income accounted for 42 percent.) However, when male earnings were substituted for female earnings and combined with dual earner, R^2 changed to 0.70. Male earnings accounted for 70 percent of the variation; that is almost the equivalent of male and female income combined.

The effect of male versus female income was also estimated in relation to the four major study hypotheses: parental SES, age and marital status at first birth, and current marital status. As illustrated in Table 9, when male earnings were entered into a regression equation, 75 percent of the variance in current economic well–being was explained. Female income does little to explain the impact of the major predictors of poverty. It explains only 10 percent of the variance. Female income was inversely associated with parental SES. The reliance of a female's parents on government assistance was inversely associated with her present income. Her current income dropped $370 if her parents were on assistance ($p =$ 0.04). This again demonstrates the interaction of ethnicity because those who were African American (parents and sample participants) tended to be unmarried and, therefore, relied more heavily on government assistance. The regression analysis suggested that labor market segmentation by gender rather than current marital status was really behind the differences in economic well–being and percent of poverty level for females. It simply does not make economic sense for many of the females in the study to work, especially when child care, proportionate reductions in subsidies, and work–related expenses are considered. A female's income had little effect in the regression model whether they were the sole earner or when combined with a male partner's earnings in the same family. As can be seen in Table 10, the males earned from 37 percent to 196 percent higher than the females.

At the educational level of the females in the study (non college degreed), their earning power is more limited than for males with comparable education. As noted by Ellwood (1993), it is not economically advantageous for a women to work unless she can make $8.00 an hour and receives health and child care. Only one female in the present study earned over this amount and she operated a daycare facility in her home: by doing so her work-related expenses and child care costs were eliminated. As Table 11 at the end of the chapter illustrates, many of the employed women were working for less than one dollar an hour greater than what they could receive on government assistance if they stayed home. Moreover, this figure does not take into account the potential government entitlement for housing, medical, and their work-related expenses.

Reporting Limitations

A final validity issue is the reliability of the reported information by the females. An important consideration is that the respondents are retrospectively reporting certain items. Selective retention as well as perceptual reorientation of what is remembered, i.e. memory changes, are well documented interview research problems (cf. Babbie 1992; Bernard 1988). For example, Bernard (1988) notes two common types of retrospective reporting concerns. First, is the potential for imprecise reporting because of selective retention or memory errors, such as the potentially unreliable reporting of the correct amount of government aid or number of times a child was taken to a health practitioner. A second type of problem that can occur is telescoping or perceptual reorientation wherein the individual may distort the length of time associated with certain conditions such as the amount of time on AFDC or other life events.

In addition to retrospective reporting issues, cultural norms may also constrain a person and create reporting imprecision. It is well documented in the literature that an informant may feel pressure to give an answer which he/she thinks the researcher would like to hear, or which conforms to mainstream behavioral norms (cf. the well known example of the Arizona garbage dump project on alcoholism in Macionis 1995). Pressure to give the normative response is especially great when status differences are present (cf. Milgram's well known research on obedience in Babbie 1995). This was certainly the case in the present study, given the medical environment in which the women were originally interviewed and the university-related association of the second research endeavor.

Because of the retrospective reporting difficulties, some information, such as previous or parental income levels, were not assessed. It was felt that the respondents might feel pressured to give a response even when they were not sure of an answer. Current income levels appeared to be reported relatively accurately. Most women readily answered how much they or their spouses earned hourly or netted weekly. Such questions were asked in the context of strategies for making ends meet and paying the bills. Most of the women responded with pride regarding their family's current earnings without hesitation during the overall discussion of earnings, subsidies and employment benefits. In consultation with a CPA, each reported income was converted to an appropriate net/gross income for analysis purposes.

Generalizability of the Findings

A major threat to external validity for longitudinal studies is the characteristics of the initial participants who are lost to follow-up. Those who are more likely to be lost to follow-up may well be the tails of the distribution who are highest or lowest at risk for the outcome. For example, those who are most likely to be persistently poor are more likely to move frequently and less likely to leave forwarding information. Those at the other end of the distribution, who are no longer in poverty, would be less likely to have received recent medical care at Oklahoma Memorial Hospital or the Family Medicine Clinics and thus have a current contact telephone of their medical records. Secondly, these women have greater financial resources with which to relocate to another area owing to a job or marriage. As a result of loss to follow-up, the present study contained a small number of persons compared to the original sample size and those persons were not randomly selected form the original study participant sample. This makes generalizations about the experiences of the Welfare Dependent, Cyclers, Combiners, Temporary Poverty, and Self Sufficient groups of women to other persons in poverty more difficult.

Generalizability across persons, places, and times is a major challenge to all researchers of human behavior. The sample seems typical of lower to lower-middle class European and African Americans who deliver their infants at primary care obstetrical clinics serving both low-and-middle-class populations. Importantly, the findings of the present study follow the trends noted in state and national level data such as those of the US Bureau of the Census and Oklahoma State Department of Health. While loss because of follow-up is a major problem in such longitudinal research, nevertheless, it is the most appropriate method by which to document the heterogeneous and dynamic profile of women in poverty. Additional research efforts will assess whether the findings of the present study are generalizable to other persons in poverty.

Findings of the Study

Introduction

The statistical analysis reveals several important findings that warrant further discussion. The multivariate analysis demonstrated the impact of marital status on reducing the effects of the earlier risks for poverty that were investigated. The effects of early pregnancy, marital status at the time of first pregnancy, and parental socioeconomic status may have initial consequences for a woman, but their impact is mitigated later in life if she marries. The findings regarding the impact of marital status in relation to a female's economic well-being reflect cultural and economic constraints in the United States regarding wages, career choices, and availability of a stable marriage partner. These constraints were discussed by many women during their interviews and were corroborated in the statistical analysis. The three constraints which have the greatest consequences for women are discussed in the following section. The first area is the differences in marital status between ethnic groups, both at first birth and later in life. Second, the differences in income between male and female earners need to be addressed. Finally, the findings regarding the effect of educational intervention strategies and the structure of government entitlement raises important questions for welfare reform discussion.

Finding One: Differences in Marriage Rates by Ethnicity

Nationally in 1960, 34 percent of European Americans aged 14 to 24 were married, compared to 26 percent of African Americans in the same age group. By 1990 the marriage rate had dropped to only 13 percent for African Americans and 27 percent for European Americans, a ratio of 1:2. For those ages 25 to 44, the corresponding 1960 marriage rates were 85 percent for European Americans and 65 percent for African Americans. By 1990 these rates had declined to 75 percent and 45 percent respectively (Wilson 1987). The marriage rate in the present sample follows these national trends. Of the 15 pregnancies that occurred by age

18, only one African American was married, compared to nearly all (7 of 8) of the European American females being married.

How can the differences in marital status between ethnic groups be explained? While numerous behavioral and structural reasons may be associated with these trends, three factors deserve special attention. Differences in marital status by ethnicity are influenced by what Lancaster (1989) and Wilson (1987) refer to as the lack of marriageable male partners for African American females. Specifically, the reduction in the number of desirable mates is influenced by: (1) reduction in employment rates for young African American males, coupled with the marriage disincentive associated with government assistance, (2) rising incarceration rates, and (3) differential homicide rates. Each of these limits the number of potential "marriageable male partners" and makes other parental investment strategies, on the part of both females and their partners, necessary. As Lancaster states:

> The facultative polyandry rate has been driven by two factors: the creation of a large pool of underemployed males because of the precipitous drop in demand for unskilled labor, and the removal of large numbers of men from the potential marriage pool by jail, military service, drug addiction, and higher death rates from violence and risk taking (1989b: 69).

Effects of Unemployment on the Differences in Marriage Rates
Employment rates in Oklahoma differ by age category and ethnicity as they do at the national level. The unemployment rate in Oklahoma for African Americans is 15.1 percent, the highest of all ethnic groups. The ratio of unemployed African Americans to European Americans is 3:1, that is higher than the national average of 2:1. The rate of unemployment for African Americans has increased (from 11.8%) in Oklahoma during the last six years by nearly one-fourth, to 15.1 percent (Statistical Abstract of Oklahoma: 1995).

Unemployment rates differ nationally across ethnic groups as well. Labor market segmentation by age and ethnicity has had serious consequences for all poor persons. Nationally, unemployment ratios of African Americans to European Americans did not reach 2:1 until 1954.

Before that there was actually greater African American employment, although in the lowest wage sector. Unemployment ratios today have remained above 2:1 every year, and are the highest in the south and southwest regions of the U.S. (Devine and Wright (1993:72). By 1984, only 58 percent of African American young adult males were employed. Moreover, only 34 percent of African Americans aged 18 to 19 were employed, compared to 70 percent of their European American counterparts (Wilson 1991:72). These are prime marriage–age males for the women who give birth as teens. Logic dictates that, given the differences in employment ratios, the partners of the African American women in this study would be at least twice as likely to be unemployed at first birth than the European American males in the same age cohort. Under such circumstances, it does not make sense for African American males and females to marry if the male is unemployed. The rational choice is to remain unmarried and eligible for government assistance, in spite of cultural rules to the contrary.

It is of interest that the women (three African American and one European American) in the present study who gave birth at age 17 or younger and did not marry, reported their first partner to be unemployed or in school in most cases. Those women who gave birth at age 17 or younger and married (four European American), reported their partners employed in almost every instance. Their employment ranged from being a chef, nurses aide, working at a recycling company, and in the military. Those who gave birth at 18 or older, were married to partners who were employed in their own businesses, or worked in service industries such as meat cutters, janitors and grocery store sackers. On the other hand, the partners of those 18 year olds who did not marry generally were unemployed or in school two-thirds of the time.

The age and composition of the pool of potential partners who are already poor and therefore cannot support a partner and child is also growing—especially among marriage age African Americans. In the nation's central cities in 1977, the overall ethnic makeup was 30.3 percent European American, 23.9 percent African American, and 21.8 percent Hispanic. However, the number of central city African Americans aged fourteen to twenty-four rose 78 percent from 1960 to 1970 compared to only 23 percent for European Americans (Wilson 1987:47-48). In

Oklahoma, the percent of poverty for those who are age 25 to 34 is 42 and 31 percent for African American and European American respectively. Among those age 15 to 24, the percent of poverty shows greater disparity; it is 67 percent for African American and only 13 percent for European American (Statistical Abstract of Oklahoma: 1995).

Incarceration Effects on the Differences in Marriage Rates

Differential rates of incarceration are the second factor that might explain the differences in marriage between ethnic groups. The ethnic composition of Oklahoma is 82.3 percent European American and 7.4 African American (Bureau of the Census: 1990b), yet the ethnic makeup in prison is disproportionately skewed toward being African American. Connely found that the male prison population in Oklahoma was 62 percent European American and 30 percent African American—a rate of four times higher than the general African American population (1994:82). Arrest rates for African Americans are twice those of European Americans (Bureau of Justice Statistics 1994:378). Since 1980 the incarceration rate for European Americans has declined by around 10 percent but it has increased by 10 percent for African Americans.

The ages of those incarcerated correlate highly with the prime marriage age. The 1994 *Sourcebook of Criminal Justice* indicates that those ages 16 to 21 make up 8.2 percent of the population nationally, but one quarter - a 3:1 ratio - of the prison population. Correspondingly, 19 to 24 year olds make up nine percent of the general population but represent an additional one quarter of the prison population (1994:377). Seventy percent of those in prison are in their 20s. Cultural rules of hypergamy make this the very age group of culturally desirable marriage partners for the women in the sample who had their first child by 18. It is also the very age group that is disproportionately represented in the prison population.

Much of the increase in incarceration rates is for nonviolent offenses, especially illegal substance possession and trafficking (Connely 1994:83). The overall incarceration rate for such offenses, male and female combined, is 17.4 percent for Oklahoma and 21.5 nationally (Camp in Sandhu 1994:19).[1] In the present sample of 47 women, two had drug– related convictions. Four reported their partners had been or currently were incarcerated. Two of the incarcerated males were partners of the females who had been arrested; both were convicted for drug possession or trafficking. The other incarcerated partners were convicted of driving under the influence and burglary. Offenses such as those committed by the men and women in the present study comprise half of the convictions of the prison population. Those arrested for drugs make up 17.4 percent, DUI 13.5 percent, and burglary 14.8 percent. Burglary and poverty often go hand-in-hand; those who were arrested for burglary reported that 58 percent of the time the need for money was the reason they committed the offense (Bureau of Justice Statistics 1994).

The disproportionate age and composition of the prison population, coupled with the dramatic increase in nonviolent offenders, provide a second cause for the differences in marriage rates found in the present study. One possible solution for both male and female nonviolent offenders is alterative punitive measures to incarceration. For example, one of the convicted females interviewed in the course of this research was required to do community service in lieu of incarceration. In addition, she was required to actively pursue employment and to report her efforts. These and other alternatives to living behind prison bars may be more beneficial to reducing poverty. In Lexington, Oklahoma's state prison, such alternative programs are currently being tested (Sandhu 1994:47). The alternatives would allow both male and female nonviolent offenders to remain employed or in school with supervision, to pay restitution through community service, and to live at home under house arrest or with probation officer supervision. Such alternatives would increase the pool of potential *marriageable* males.

Homicide Effects on the Differences in Marriage Rates
High homicide rates for young African American males are a third factor that may help explain differences in marriage rates between ethnic groups. The rates for those ages 15 to 19 have been increasing since 1965. The highest rate of homicide, however, is for those ages 20 to 24 (19 percent); the prime marriageable age group. They are followed by those ages 15 to 19 (13 percent) and 25 to 29 (15 percent) (Bureau of Justice Statistics 1994:333). These age groups comprise nearly half (46 percent) of all homicides nationally.

To summarize, nearly half of homicide *victims* are between the ages of 15 to 29. Males make up over three-fourths (77 percent) of the homicide victims. Moreover, African Americans make up one-half (51 percent) of the victims (Connely 1994). There is a homicide rate of 184.1 males per 100,000 for African American males age 18 to 24. The disproportionate incidence of homicide among marriage age males appears to be yet another reason for the differences in marriage rates between ethnic groups. Taken together, increasing ratios of underemployed and unemployed marriage age males, increasing incarceration rates, especially among nonviolent offenders, a precipitous rise in homicide rates, and cultural rules of who is a desirable mate have quite literally shrunken the ranks of the male marriage pool, especially for young, non-degreed females of color.

Finding Two: Occupational Segregation and Income

The second important finding of the present research is the income disparity between male and females. Marriage rates would not correlate highly with poverty were it not for female occupational segregation. The median wage in Oklahoma according to the 1990 census data was $18,500 for European American males compared to $8,788 for their female counterparts. The median income for African American males was $10,983 compared to $7,117 for their female counterparts. In other words, for every dollar a European American male earned in 1990, an African American male earned 9¢, a European American female earned 47¢, and an African American female earned 38¢ (Figure 15).

The association of female wages and poverty becomes even clearer when looking at household census data. The median income for households in Oklahoma was $30,168 for European American married couple families compared to $12,021 for their female headed counterparts. The median income for African American married couple families was $18,511 compared to $7,345 for their female headed counterparts. African American female heads of families fared the poorest. For every dollar a European American married couple household earned, an African American married couple earned 61¢, a European

American female headed family with children earned 39¢, and an African American female headed family with children earned only 24¢ (Figure 14).

A comparison of income across ethnicity, gender, and marital status was difficult in the present study given the small number of cases when subdivided. Only two African American females were currently married and both husbands were high wage earners. Their net income averaged $1,641 per month, or around $20,000 a year. Five of the African American women were working. They brought home an average of $727 a month or $8,724 a year. Among those of European American ethnicity, the employed males earned an average of $1,236 a month or $14,840 per year; whereas the 18 females averaged $807 a month or $9,684 a year. Stated another way, for every dollar an African American male earned, a European American male in this sample only earned 75¢; a finding contrary to income averages for the general population. Females did not fare well in relation to the males, regardless of their ethnicity. The European American female earned 49¢ and the African American female earned 44¢. There was one striking deviation from the state level data: the two African American females who did marry, were much better off economically than the average European American female who married. The income findings of the present study only partially mirrored the trends at the state level. The disparities by gender were comparable, but differences occurred when the present sample was stratified by both ethnicity and gender.

The gender differences across both ethnic groups were striking. The net income for males in the sample averaged $14,808, while for females it averaged $8,052, regardless of ethnicity. In other words, the females in the study earned an average of 52¢ for every $1.00 earned by the males in the study; that is, the men on average earned between $1.37 to $2.13 for every $1.00 a female earned (see Table 10).

As noted earlier, the income disparity by gender found in the present study is comparable to state level data and national trends. These findings support the view that non-degreed females are concentrated in low wage positions that keep them at or near the poverty level, even when employed. This was true even when a sample, such as the present one, was comprised of predominantly low wage earners, rather than the general, state population. Prevailing cultural norms distinguish between the social prestige associated with certain occupations and economic compensation. Women have traditionally been employed in helping and service-related positions which are culturally viewed as conferring intrinsic and social satisfaction at the cost of economic remuneration. I am reminded of the story found in many Social Stratification text books (cf. Beeghley 1996):

> On a cold snowy day in New York, the secretaries in the high rise office building send cat calls to the workers below. Hey guys, it's 72 degrees in here. They reply, Hey girls, it's $17.00 an hour out here.

Finding Three: Cultural Rules Regarding Educational Achievement

A third important finding of the study was the relationship between occupations, gender roles and educational choices. High school graduation rates have essentially evened out across ethnic groups. According to the 1990 census data for Oklahoma, 85, 86, 82, and 84 percent respectively of European American males and females and their respective African American cohorts ages 25 to 34 have graduated from high school. However, important differences begin to emerge at the college level (Figure 3). In the 25 to 34 age cohort, 21 percent of European American, but only 12 percent of African American males, have completed college. Likewise, 20 percent of European American and 12 percent of African American females have done so.

Poverty and education closely correspond in Oklahoma and elsewhere. Among those in poverty in Oklahoma, 44 percent of those who are African American and 19 percent of European American do not have a high school education, while only 19 and 6 percent respectively who have some college education are poor. If one can finish a college degree, poverty chances are greatly reduced. Only 5 percent of African Americans and 2 percent of European Americans in poverty have a college degree (Statistical Abstract of Oklahoma 1995:297).

Almost all the women in the present study had completed high school, regardless of whether they dropped out while pregnant, contrary to the findings of Furstenburg (1991, 1992) and Upchurch and McCarthy (1990). The findings of the present research probably reflect recent effects of special programs that are increasingly becoming available to teen mothers. The findings also likely reflect the effect of AFDC regulations that require women to attend school or to seek employment if their children are over two years of age. This regulation has enabled the women to complete high school and, in some cases, advanced training. As yet, no one in this study has completed a Bachelor's degree. Even those who acquired some advanced training, e.g. Vo-Tech, did not benefit from it to the degree that was initially expected. Many who were interviewed had not thought about the marketability of the field they selected. Others did not receive sufficient training to acquire market-competitive skills. No women were currently employed in fields in which they were trained. For example, many women took courses at business colleges or Vo-Tech but did not seek and/or secure related employment afterwards. Several women mentioned that business colleges especially tended to capitalize on government assistance requirements in order to generate a student pool. This is reminiscent of the landlords mentioned earlier who receive inflated Section 8 rental reimbursements from the government.

Most women reported future educational interest in fields of health care and other helping professions. Only one expressed interest in natural science, engineering, or skilled manual positions. Only two women were currently attending a university, one in psychology, and the other planned to specialize in forensics. Two women had already completed an Associate's degree. One of them majored in accounting but could not find a related job because of lack of experience; she worked as a teacher's aide. The other woman has returned to school in order to complete a Bachelor's degree and is furthering her interests in psychology. She was presently working in retail for low wages.

Conclusions

Adaptation Strategies and the Impingement of Cultural Rules
This paper began with a discussion of how cultural rules that guide behavior in one situation can have long-term consequences. As first noted by Mazess (1975), there are tensions between options a woman and man may choose. While certain strategies such as educational choices, marrying young, or choosing instead to rely on government assistance, may be adaptive in the short term, they may have long-term costs.

These choices do not occur in isolation, but are constrained and shaped by the cultural rules that shape the economic and political system. The economic and political structure, also culturally sculpted, may require ideological and behavioral adjustments in *individual* decision making that might be in tension with or limit one's ability to initiate certain adaptive strategies.

In this sense human behavior is a consequence of social relations and political relations that affect biological and group functioning. Often these social relations are unequal and are generated from beyond the boundaries of the local system by a political and economic system upon which the group becomes dependent (Thomas 1994). Perhaps the most important consequence for the present study was the structure of government entitlement. The eligibility requirements created a circumstance wherein the adaptive choice, unless the male partner was economically stable, was for the female to remain unmarried. Lancaster (1989b:67) states:

> The primary determinant of family formation and parental investment strategies should be the needs of women for access to resources to rear children . . . using this perspective, female headed, single parent households are viewed as created not by default of male interest, but rather by adaptations to particular distributions of social and physical resources in the environment.

An important consideration is the extent to which female headship may be an accommodative response to the distribution of resources, and may be adaptive at one level but have associated costs at another. For example, a female with children may be less able to attract a future marriage partner or to accumulate material resources. A second consideration is whether what is adaptive or most efficient in the short term, such as female headship, may be maladaptive in the long-term.

Prevailing Cultural Rules Regarding Marriage
The choice not to marry when first pregnant may be what Mazess (1975) and others refer to as an accommodation (external conformity) rather than a true adaptation. The reasons this practice results in an accommodation strategy are several fold. First, most women when interviewed stated they did not intend to get pregnant but did so because they did not use contraception or used it inconsistently or improperly. Second, most of the women expressed a desire to marry, and third, they expressed the desire to work. These are two strong cultural rules in our society that are limited by external constraints for many women. When women in the study were asked why they did not marry the partner with whom they became pregnant, the reasons varied. Many felt they were too young, were not "in love" with the partner, their partners were not willing to make a commitment, or felt they and their partners could not "make it on their own." Thus, some chose not to marry although many would eventually like to if they found the "right and committed" partner; they instead relied on government assistance.

The marriage disincentive associated with government assistance made these women initially better off economically than those who chose to marry but were concentrated in low wage or entry occupational positions. In the long run, however, the married women tended to move into better positions because of their husband's (if employed) greater earning power.

Prevailing Cultural Rules Regarding Work
The needs of those who are on assistance are taken care of, but only if they remain poor and unmarried. Thus, while they may choose to marry, the choice only makes sense if the partner can earn sufficient wages to

compensate for the provisions of the government. Most women expressed a desire to work rather than to rely on government assistance. A woman may choose to work, but this decision makes sense only if she can earn enough to make up for what the government would provide if she stayed dependent. The built in work disincentive makes this choice a difficult one and may appear adaptive at first choice, but can have long–term maladaptive costs because her occupational choices may not result in sufficient economic remuneration. Thus, many women are in a double–bind situation. Government dependency creates intense cultural pressure for an unmarried women to eventually begin to work, both because of informal group pressure and the formal regulations of government assistance. This is true, given present welfare reform regulations, even if she can find only a minimum wage position. The net result is that by choosing to work, she may reduce her income and benefits compared to what she once received from her surrogate caretaker, the government. Figure 16 shows the actual wages of female earners in the sample and subtracts what each female could potentially receive from the government depending on family size, were she not to work. The estimates take into account only AFDC and food stamps. The surprising finding was that no woman gained a net economic benefit of more than $2.00 an hour by working, although the women reported gains in non-economic benefits in terms of prestige, independence and self–esteem.

An issue one might explore is the relationship between occupational wages and gender. In Oklahoma, the average weekly earnings in construction in 1990 were $447 a week, or $10.88 an hour. In commercial machinery, metal fabrications and manufacturing, the average salaries ranged from $10.50 to $12.00 an hour. However, some interesting differences emerge when one compares traditionally female occupations to those traditionally male occupations just mentioned. The average 1990 wages in apparel and textiles was half that for construction workers. In Oklahoma workers in the apparel and textile industry earned an average of only $202 weekly or $5.65 an hour. The situation was bleaker in retail. Retail workers in Oklahoma earned $5 to $6 an hour and averaged only $191 per week compared to $384 for wholesale workers (Affirmative Action Labor Reports for Oklahoma: 1990).

African American females in Oklahoma and elsewhere are concentrated in service occupations (35 percent compared to 18 percent European American); whereas, European American females tend to be concentrated in administrative support (32 percent compared to 24 percent African American). Others of both ethnic groups are working in sales (around 10 percent). These occupational categories are the pink collar trades. They are traditionally defined as support or service positions and pay at considerably lower wages. They are also traditionally occupied by females such as those women interviewed in the present study.

Concluding Summary

There are competing tensions between the political and economic structuring of government entitlement, women's occupational rewards and educational choices, and cultural rules that say it is good to work and to be married. Because of the tension between the rule of being married, the structure of government assistance, and the available occupations for themselves and their potential partners, women in the present study sometimes deviated from the cultural rule and did not marry. Instead, they had long–term relationships, sometimes exceeding eight years, with partners who made visits and fathered the women's children. Even with the competing cultural rules of marriage, occupational rewards and government entitlement, most women expressed a future desire to marry and to work. Figure 16 illustrates the net dollars per hour females are earning, compared to what they could receive on government assistance.

Those who did marry were economically, though not always emotionally, better off, even if they stayed home as homemakers. Many of the married women expressed a desire to be full time homemakers and stay home with their children rather than send them to day care or sitters. Others felt trapped in marriages with husbands upon whom they were dependent. The full-time homemakers had weighed the economic considerations of child care, transportation and other work-related costs with the amount of earnings they could produce. Because of the low wages and desire to raise a family, most married women—even those who had worked before becoming pregnant—stayed at home. Only 23 percent of the sample consisted of dual earners.

Of those who chose government assistance over marriage at the time of first pregnancy, all but three completed high school, either with government or kinship assistance. Were these women to have made wiser choices regarding advanced training programs while on government assistance, they would be financially better off and the advantages of choosing government assistance, more adaptive. Many, however, completed their education with a high school diploma and others took advanced training in fields in which they could not earn much money or in which the training, perhaps at a business college, did not benefit them in terms of securing related employment. Different educational choices are only a partial solution. As more persons with college degrees enter the job market, fewer positions will be available. As competition for such positions increases, others will dip below the poverty level to replace those who have left. If more women were able to complete a Bachelor's degree or receive training in high wage manual positions while on government assistance, the adaptive advantages would be greater. Those in the study who did go beyond high school opted for training in low wage helping professions, rather than the high wage manual and technical fields.

The competing tensions between the work disincentive associated with the structure of government assistance and the cultural rule that it is good to work and not to be on the dole, warrant some concluding comments. Several of the women would have been financially better off remaining welfare dependent. Some may, in fact, become so again unless they can manage to "hang on" once their government-supported child care and housing subsidies are substantially reduced or eliminated. If the women can hold on long enough, around three years, they can earn up to $7.00 per hour based on the work history of the present sample. The new welfare reform regulations will create a new working poor class of women such as those in the present study who are caught between minimum wage and the $7.00 an hour threshold.

As noted above, the women were presently working for an average of $40 to $60 more per week than they would receive from the government. However, this figure takes into account only their potential

AFDC and food stamp entitlements, not housing, medical, and work-related expenses such as meals, transportation, clothing and child care. Were these expenses taken into account, they would more than negate the $40 to $60 more dollars the women currently earn above what they could receive on government assistance. It is a big leap for a woman to leave the government safety net behind, although many women have done so and many more will be required to do so as a result of welfare reform. Those women in the present study who were no longer on government assistance expressed considerable concern about upcoming disproportionate reductions in the benefits on which they had learned to depend.

A final consideration concerns divorced females and the structure of child support payments from the noncustodial parent. Most of the women in the study were not receiving child support payment from the biological father. Those who did had it subtracted, dollar for dollar, from their AFDC payment. Consequently, both families were poorer because the money was transferred from the biological father and his newly created family to the female, and that proportionate amount was reduced from her aid. The resources transferred from one family leave it poorer and do not financially benefit the second family at child support levels commensurate with the earnings of the men in this study. The rational choice would be for the father to make informal contributions to the child's welfare if the parents have a cooperative relationship. But most men were not paying child support, regardless of whether it was awarded.

For those who continued to rely on government assistance and not to marry or to gain training in high wage occupations, there were long–term maladaptive costs because the structure of government assistance keeps one at the poverty level. A concluding question is why government entitlements are structured as such. Prevailing cultural rules reflect that Americans do not want anyone to go hungry. Yet, if someone is getting a handout, Americans do not want them to enjoy material comforts; that satisfaction is reserved for the workers in society. Moreover, we do not want those who *are* getting a handout to double dip. Either they stay dependent or pick themselves up by the bootstraps and make it on their own like the rest of productive members of America. Welfare reform will shift those persons who stay welfare dependent onto other agencies, both public and private. Occupational segregation by gender, work related expenses for women with children, and contraction of the manufacturing sector for men without advanced degrees make this "work fare" cultural rule impractical. Yet the women in this study looked forward to the day when they could be independent of Uncle Sam and, as wage earners, buy the things they wanted for themselves and their children like "other" members of society.

In addition, most women interviewed expressed the desire to marry if they could find a suitable, "stable" man. Many women married at first birth, whether or not it was the economically rational choice, because they were in love. These women in the long–term are financially better off; yet the vast majority have substituted dependency on Uncle Sam for dependency on a male earner's wages, without which they, too, would join the ranks of the poor female householders.

The disparity in income has led to a stratification system in Oklahoma and elsewhere that is increasingly based on family structure, ethnicity and gender. In an increasingly technologically complex society, greater educational attainment is needed in order to move beyond the unskilled, poverty wage level. While it is not impossible to attend school and also raise a family, and many of our university students can personally attest to accomplishing such a challenge, they can likewise attest to its difficulty. Is it then no surprise that female single parents, especially those of color, make up the majority of disadvantaged families in Oklahoma and the United States?

Intervention Recommendations for the Future

One: The first area of intervention is to reduce gender-related labor force segregation by occupations. Labor force segmentation needs to be corrected and these adjustments can begin in the educational system. Female students can be counseled to engage in skilled technical training in areas, such as engineering and telecommunications, that will be in demand for the future. Spatial and mathematical skills need greater emphasis for women students. Cultural rules regarding pay scales for such professions as teaching, health care, clerical and retail services need to be reevaluated.

Two: The government regulations regarding education requirements for AFDC recipients must take into consideration the marketability of the educational training recipients are receiving and the corresponding number of available jobs in a post–industrial economy. The women of the present study tended to focus on health and business related areas at technical schools. Few actually completed the courses and not one woman gained employment in the field in which she received training. Provisions for educational training that will result in greater earning power for women, rather than simply meeting ADFC stipulations, need to be considered as part of the welfare reform package. Finally, provisions to obtain a Bachelor's degree as well as job placement for those on welfare is an important consideration.

Three: A national health care plan, job protection during pregnancy, and *real* pregnancy leave protection will ease some of the obstacles most frequently reported by women in this study. Not until there is a day care cooperative in every community, its costs underwritten by the corporate sector, will the biggest obstacle to most working men and women be solved—child care costs.

Four: Another intervention recommendation is the restructuring of government subsidies in order to eliminate the work and marriage disincentives. The present structure, even with welfare term limits and other changes, weakens the position of the male in the poor family by tying cash subsidies to marriage regulations. Moreover, the present structuring of entitlements, nevertheless continues to disproportionately reduce benefits to the working poor. Plans such as those in Europe, and elsewhere create guaranteed living standards, tax inducements, and other programs that enable and encourage work among the poor, but also enable them to accumulate some capital without immediately losing subsidies.

One problem with the interventions and welfare reform measures mentioned thus far is that they assume jobs at higher pay are readily available if one has gained the appropriate skill requirements, and resolved problems related to child care and transportation. That has not happened. Economic restructuring because of technological advances has eliminated many jobs and created more sophisticated and lengthy training requirements for the filling of newly created positions. Computers, e-mail, voice mail, and other advances have eliminated the need for many workers. The world economy simply does not need as many workers in a post-industrial age. Thus, new population pressures have resulted simply because there are more persons than viable positions for workers to fill. Reduction in population will relieve some poverty by reducing the number of available workers to fill positions.

Five: Therefore, perhaps one of the most important intervention strategies is the final one, that is, to make birth control measures readily available and culturally approved for all persons. Biologically driven hormonal drives are difficult to curtail, but with today's advances in artificial contraception, pregnancy can be prevented. A vision for the future is to see condom vending machines alongside soda machines and a once-a-month birth control pill available for purchase alongside Excederin and Mylanta.

Recommendations for Future Research

One: More study of the relationship between marital status and poverty needs to be conducted. Specifically, future research should compare differences in poverty between ethnic groups, while controlling for current marital status. Such a comparison was a challenge in the present study because of the small sample size, especially for married African American females and males.

Two: Discussion regarding the confounding of ethnicity in poverty research should be explored. Some factors once attributed to ethnicity may instead be socioeconomic, or a result of structural causes such as economic restructuring and the regulation of government entitlement.

Three: Finally, more longitudinal poverty research is needed. Difficulties associated with such studies are numerous. Nevertheless, they provide important insight into the heterogenous and dynamic makeup of the many faces of poverty, faces such as those of the women whose lives are chronicled in this study.

NOTES

1. Women comprise 12 percent of the Oklahoma prison population, leading the nation in female incarceration rates. African American females comprise 3.8 percent of the Oklahoma population but comprise 40 percent of the female prison population (Moon et. al 1994:23). The rate for females has doubled in the last five years largely because of drug related offenses. During the last decade drug related arrests for females have risen at twice the rate of for males—a 307 percent increase as compared to 147 percent for males (Sandhu 1994:19). Roughly one-third (34.7 percent) of all females in Oklahoma prisons were arrested on drug related charges.

Table 9 Regression Coefficients of the Independent Determinates of Poverty: Full Model

Independ. Variables	Model One %AFDC				Model Two Subsidized Income				Model Three Male Income				Model Four Female Income			
	b	S.E.	stb	p	b	S.E.	stb	p	b	S.E.	stb	p	b	S.E.	stb	p
Parental SES	12.16	2.93	0.421	0.0002	311.86	148.83	0.28	0.04	34.05	144.21	0.02	0.81	-370	182.55	-0.33	0.04
MS 1st birth	-6.58	3.14	-0.26	0.04	-203.89	157.14	-0.21	0.20	80.04	152.25	0.06	0.60	-11.15	-0.05	-0.01	0.95
Age 1st birth	-0.16	0.42	-0.04	0.69	-0.42	2164	0.00	0.98	-24.58	20.97	-0.10	0.024	-26.97	-1.02	-0.16	0.31
Current MS	-7.79	2.94	-0.32	0.01	-250.27	144.47	-0.27	0.09	1157.69	139.99	0.83	0.0001	-179.98	-0.09	-0.19	0.33
R^2	0.65				0.37				0.75				0.10			
R^2 adj	0.62				0.31				0.72				0.01			
N	46				46				46				46			

Model One: Proportion of Adult Life on AFDC
Model Two: Total Subsidized Income
Model Three: Male net Earned Income
Model Four: Female Net Earned Income

Table 10 Male to Female Earning Ratio

Earners Only

Group#	W P	C Y C	C O M	T P	S S	A V ALL
Female Income: Net	737	724	791	918	866	671
Male Income: Net	0	1540	1171	1328	1186	1234
TEN(M)TEN(F)	0	2.13	1.48	1.45	1.37	1.84
TEN(F)/TSI	0.64	1.25	2.96	9.56	INFIN	
Total Subs Income (TSI)	1158	581	267	96	0	

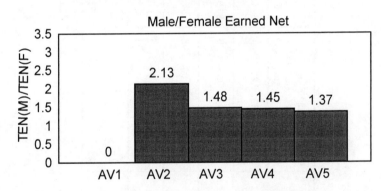

Male/Female Earned Net

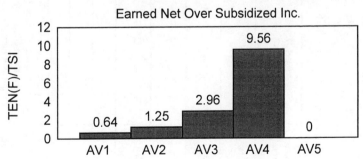

Earned Net Over Subsidized Inc.

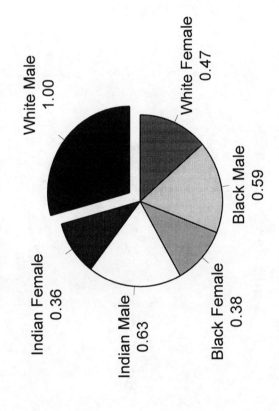

**Median Income in Oklahoma
Cents Per Dollar: 1990**

White Male 1.00

White Female 0.47

Black Male 0.59

Black Female 0.38

Indian Male 0.63

Indian Female 0.36

Figure 14

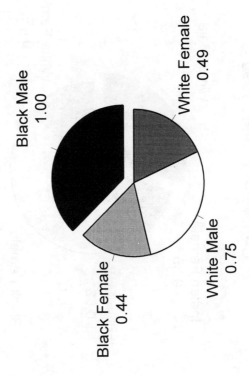

Median Income Sample Respondents
Cents Per Dollar: 1994

Black Male
1.00

White Female
0.49

White Male
0.75

Black Female
0.44

Figure 15

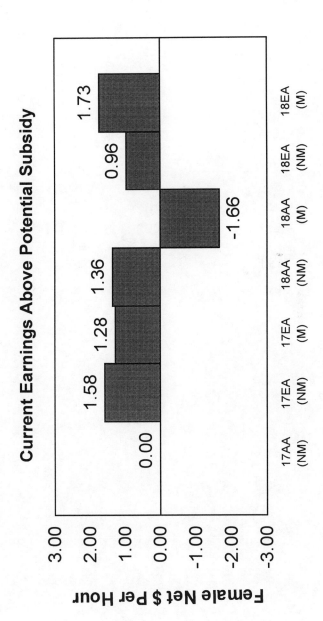

Figure 16

Appendix

Explanation of Variables

Group #	=	Poverty Type Classification
ID #	=	Interview Case Number
Months to 9/95	=	Females Age Converted to Months
Ethnicity	=	Ethnic Origin
SES	=	Were the Females Parents on Government Assistance
Age at First Birth	=	Females Age at First Birth
Marital - 1st Birth	=	Females Marital Status at First Birth
Divorced	=	Was Female Ever Divorced from any Marriage Partner
Current MS	=	Is Female Currently Married
# in family	=	Current Number of Persons in Family
Appropriations $	=	Hypothetical Government Entitlement Based on Female and Current Number of Dependents
Female Net = Approp $/m	=	Monthly Net Earned Income Minus Potential Government Entitlements
Female Net = Approp $/h	=	Hourly Net Earned Income Minus Potential Government Entitlements

Other Income	=	Includes Tips, Bonuses and Child Support
Female Income: Gross	=	Earned Income Before Taxes
Net	=	Earned Income After Taxes and other Employee Deductions
Male Income: Gross	=	Earned Income Before Taxes
Net	=	Earned Income After Taxes and other Employee Deductions
Total Earned Gross (TEG)	=	Combined Earned Income
Total Earned Net (TEN)	=	Combined Earned Income After Deductions
Health Care Coverage	=	Does Family Have Health Care Coverage
AFDC	=	Monthly AFDC Payments
Stamps	=	Amount of Monthly Food Stamps
Housing (HS)	=	Amount of Housing Subsidy
SSI	=	Disability and Social Security Payments
Total Subs Income (TSI)	=	Monthly Total Subsidized Income
Tot Subs Income - HS	=	Monthly Cash Subsidy (minus house subsidy)
TEN + Subs	=	Monthly Net Earned Income Plus Government Subsidies
TEN + Subs - HS	=	Monthly Earned Net Income Plus Cash Subsidies (minus house subsidy)
House Payment (HP	=	Family's Monthly House Payment or Co-payment
Who Pays House Payment	=	By Whom is House Payment Paid
Child Care Cost (CC)	=	Monthly Amount of Child Care
TEN + Subs - HP	=	Monthly Net Earned Income Plus Government Subsidies Minus House Payment
TEN + Subs - HS -HP	=	Monthly Net Earned Income Plus Government Subsidies (minus house subsidy) Minus House Payment

TEN + Subs - HS -HP - CC		=	(Referred to as Useable Income) Monthly Net Earned Income Plus Government Subsidies (minus house subsidy) Minus House Payment Minus Child Care Cost
TEG + Subs - HS		=	Monthly Earned Gross Income Plus Cash Subsidies (minus house subsidy)
Poverty Level (PL)		=	1995 Monthly Government Income Poverty Level for Current Number in Family
(TEG + Subs)/PL		=	Percent of Poverty Level Total Earned Gross Income Plus Government Subsidies
(TEN + Subs)/PL		=	Percent of Poverty Level Total Earned Net Income Plus Government Subsidies
(TEN + Subs - HS)/PL		=	Percent of Poverty Level Total Earned Net Income Plus Government Subsidies (minus house subsidy)
(TEN + Subs - HP)/PL		=	Percent of Poverty Level Total Earned Net Income Plus Government Subsidies (minus house payment)
(TEN + Subs - HS - HP -CC)/PL		=	Percent of Poverty Level for Useable Income
Age	Month	=	Female Age in Months
Medicaid	# of Times	=	Number of Periods on Medicaid
	Month	=	Proportion of Time Female was on Medicaid
	%	=	Percent of Time Female was on Medicaid
Stamps # of Times		=	Number of Periods on Stamps
	Month	=	Proportion of Time Female was on Stamps

	%	=	Percent of Time Female was on Stamps
AFDC	# of Times	=	Number of Periods on AFDC
	Month	=	Proportion of Time Female was on AFDC
	%	=	Percent of Time Female was on AFDC
Housing	Month	=	Proportion of Time Female was on Housing
	%	=	Percent of Time Female was on Housing
SSI	Month	=	Proportion of Time Female was on SSI
	%	=	Percent of Time Female was on SSI

References

Abell, Troy
1989   Investigation of the Etiology of Intrauterine Growth
        Retardation (Low Birth Weights) and Premature Births.
        Unpublished document. University of Oklahoma Health
        Sciences Center.
1992   Low Birth Weight, Intrauterine Growth-Retarded, and
        Pre-Term Infants. *Human Nature* 3(4):335-378, New York:
        Walter de Gruyter, Inc.

Abell, Troy and Larry Lyon
1979   Do the Differences Make a Difference? An Empirical
        Evaluation of the Culture of poverty in the United States.
        American Ethnologist 6:(3)602-620.

Anderson, Elijah
1983   The Dynamics of Dependence: The Routes to
        Self-Sufficiency. Supported by a U.S. Department of Health
        and Human Services grant, contract no. HHS-100-82-0038.
1991   Neighborhood Effects on Teenage Pregnancy. Christopher S.
        Jencks and Paul E. Peterson, eds. Washington, D.C.:
        Brookings Institution. Bane, J.J., and D.T. Ellwood.

Arendall, Terry
1991   Downward Mobility. *In* The Family Experience: A Reader in
        Cultural Diversity. pp. 732-746.

Armelagos, George J., Thomas Leatherman, Mary Ryan, and Lynn
Sibley
1972   Biocultural Synthesis in Medical Anthropology. *Modual
        Anthropology.* 14:35-52.

Babbie, Earl
1995   The Practice of Social Research. Belmont, CA: Wadsworth
        Publishing Company.

Bane, Mary J.
1994   Welfare Realities: From Rhetoric to Reform. Cambridge, MA:
        Harvard University Press.

Bane, M.J., and D.T. Ellwood
1983
        Slipping into and out of Poverty: The Dynamics of Spells.
        Working paper No. 1199, National Bureau of Economic
        Research, Cambridge, MA.
1984   The Dynamics of Children's Living Arrangements. Working
        paper, supported by a U.S. Department of Health and Human
        Services grant, contract no. HHS-100-82-0038.

Beeghley, Leonard
1989   The Structure of Social Stratification in the United States.
        Boston, MA: Allyn and Bacon.

Bernard, H. Russell
1967   *The American Occupational Structure.* New York: John Wiley
        & Sons.
1988   Research Methods in Cultural Anthropology. Blau, Peter, and
        Otis Dudley, eds. Duncan, California: Sage.

Brooks, Roy L.
1990   American Race. Berkeley: University of California Press.
1992   [1990] Rethinking the American Race Problem. Berkeley and
        Los Angeles: University of California Press.

Bumpass, Larry and Sara McLanahan
1989   Unmarried Motherhood: Recent Trends, Composition and
        Black/White Differences. *Demography* 26:279-286.

Coe, Richard D.
1978   Dependency and Poverty in the Short and Long Run. *In* 5000
        American Families: Patterns of Economic Progress. G.J.
        Duncan and J.N. Morgan, eds. Vol. 6. Ann Arbor, MI:
        Institute for Social Research.

Connelly, Michael D.
1994   Basic Trends in Sentence Length and Time Served in
        Oklahoma Corrections 1900-1992. *Journal of the Oklahoma
        Criminal Justice Resource Consortium* 1:81-92.

Cutright, Phillips
1968   Occupational Inheritance: A Cross-Nation Analysis. *American
        Journal of Sociology* 73:400-416.

Cutright, P., and P. Madras
1974   AFDC and the Marital and Family Status of Ever-Married
        Women Aged 15-54: United States, 1950-1970. *Sociology and
        Social Research* 60 (April):314-27.

Devine, Joel A. And James D. Wright
1993   The Greatest of Evils: Urban Poverty and the American
        Underclass. New York: Aldine De Gruyter.

Dudley, William, ed.
1988   Poverty: Opposing Viewpoints. St. Paul, MN: Greenhaven
        Press

Duncan, Otis Dudley
1965   The Trend of Occupational Mobility in the United States.
        American Sociological Review 30:491-498.

Ellwood, David T.
1993   The Changing Structure of American Families: The Bigger
        Family Planning Issue. *Journal of the American Planning
        Association.* 59(1):3-8.

Ellwood, D.T., and M.J. Bane
1984   The Impact of AFDC on Family Structure and Living
        Arrangements. Working paper prepared for the U.S.
        Department of Health and Human Services under grant no.
        92A-82. United States, 1950-1970. *Sociology and Social
        Research* 60 (April):314-27.

Eshleman, J. Ross
1994   The Family: An Introduction. Boston: Allyn and Bacon.

Featherman, David, and Robert Hauser
1978   Opportunity and Change. New York: Academic Press.

Fitchen, Janet M.
1988   Hunger Malnutrition, and Poverty in the Contemporary United
        States: Some Observations on their Social and Cultural
        Context. *Nutrition, Obesity, Culture and Poverty.* 2:309-333.
        Great Britain: Harwood Academic Publishers GmbH.

Fricke, Tom et al.
1993   Marriage, Social Inequality, and Women's Contact with their
        Natal Families in Alliance Societies: Two Tamang Examples.
        American Anthropologist 95(2):295-419.

Frisch, R.E.
1988   Fatness and Fertility. Scientific American 258:88-95.

Furstenberg, Jr., Frank F.
1991   As the Pendulum Swings: Teenage Childbearing and Social
        Concern. *Family Relations.* 40: 127-138.
1992   Teenage Childbearing and Cultural Rationality: A Thesis in
        Search of Evidence. *Family Relations.* 41:239-243.

Geronimus, Arline T.
1992   Teenage Childbearing and Social Disadvantage Unprotected
        Discourse. *Family Relations.* 41:244-248.
1991   Teenage Childbearing and Social and Reproductive
        Disadvantage: The Evolution of Complex Questions and the
        Demise of Simple Answers. *FamilyRelations.* 463-471.

Geronimus, Arline T., and Sanders Korenman.
1993   The Socioeconomic Costs of Teenage Childbearing: Evidence
        and Interpretation. *Demography.* 30(2):281-290

Greenhalgh, Susan
1985   Is Inequality Demographically Induced? The Family Cycle
        and the Distribution of Income in Taiwan. in *American
        Anthropologist.* 87: 569-594.

Greenstein, R.
1985   Losing Faith in 'Losing Ground.' *New Republic* (March
        25):12-17.

Hill, Kim
1993   Life History Theory and Evolutionary Anthropology.
        Evolutionary Anthropology. 2(3): 78-89.

Hill, M.S.
1981   Some Dynamic Aspects of Poverty. *In* Five Thousand
        American Families: Patterns of Economic Progress 9: M.S.
        Hill, D.H. Hill, and J.N. Morgan, eds. Ann Arbor: Institute for
        Social Research, University of Michigan Press.

Hogan, D.P., N.M. Astone and E.M. Kitagawa
1985   Social and Enviornmental Factors Influencing Contraceptive
        Use among Black Adolescents. *Family Planning Perspectives*
        17:165-69.

Hogan, D.P. and E.M. Kitagawa
1983   The Impact of Social Status, Family Structure, and
        Neighborhood on the Fertility of Black Adolescents.
        American Journal of Sociology 89:825-55.

Hutter, Mark (ed.)
1991   The Family Experience: A Reader in Cultural Diversity. New
        York: Macmillan Publishing Company.

Institute for Women's Policy Research
1993   Few Welfare Mothers Fit the Stereotypes. *Research-in-Brief.*
        Institute for Women's Policy Research.

Jones, Elise, et al.
1991   Teenage Pregnancy in Developed Countries: Determinants
        and Policy Implications. *In* The Family Experience: A Reader
        in Cultural Diversity. Pp.565-588.

Kaffman, Mordecai
1977   Sexual Standards and Behavior of the Kibbutz Adolescent.
        American Journal of Orthopsychiatry. 47(2): 207-217.

Kain, Edward L.
1990   The Myth of Family Decline: Understanding Families in a
        World of Rapid Social Change. Lexington, MA: D.C. Heath
        and Company.

Kaplan, Hillard S., et al.
1995   Does Observed Fertility Maximize Fitness Among New
        Mexican Men? *Human Nature.* New York: Walter de Gruyter,
        Inc. 6(4):325-360.

Kerbo, Harold.
1996   Social Stratification and Inequality: Class Conflict in
         Historical and Comparative Perspective. New York:
         McGraw-Hill Companies, Inc.

Kessler-Harris, Alice
1982   Out to Work. Oxford: Oxford University Press.

Kohn, Melvin L.
1969   Class and Conformity: A Study in Values. 2d ed. Homewood,
         Ill: Dorsey Press.

Lancaster, Jane B.
1989a   Women in Biosocial Perspective. Sandra Morgen, ed. *In*
         Gender and Anthropology. Washington, DC: American
         Anthropological Association. Pp:95-114.
1989b   Evolutionary and Cross-Cultural Perspectives on
         Single-Parenthood. *In* Sociobiology and the Social Sciences.
         R.W. Bell and N.J. Bell, eds. Lubbock, TX: Texas Tech
         University Press.

Lancaster and Beatrix A. Hamburg, eds.
1986   School-Age Pregnancy and Parenthood: Biosocial
         Dimensions. New York: Aldine De Gruyter.

Lancaster, Jane B. and Hillard Kaplan.
1992   Human Mating and Family Formation Strategies: The Effects
         of Variability Among Males in Quality and the Allocation of
         Mating Effort and Parental Investment. Toshisada Nihida et
         al., eds. *Topics in Primatology.* 1:21-32.

Lancaster, Jane B. And Chet S. Lancaster.
1987   The Watershed: Change in Parental-Investment and
        Family-Formation Strategies in the course of Human
        Evolution. Parenting Across the Life Span: Biosocial
        Dimensions. Jane B. Lancaster, Jeanne Altmann, Alice S.
        Rossi, and Lonnie R. Sherrod, eds. New York: Aldine De
        Gruyter.

Levin, Jack and James Alan Fox
1991   Elementary Statistics in Social Research. New York:
        HarperCollins.

Low, Bobbi S.
1993   Ecological Demography: A Synthetic Focus in Evolutionary
        Anthropology. *Evolutionary Anthropology.* 1(5):177-185.

Luker, Kristin
1991   Motherhood and Morality in America *In* The Family
        Experience: A Reader in Cultural Diversity. pp. 546-564.

Lyon, Larry, Troy Abell, Elizabeth Jones and Holley Rector-Owen
1982   The National Longitudinal Surveys Data for Labor Market
        Entry: Evaluating the Small Effects of Racial Discrimination
        and the Large Effects of Sexual Discrimination. *Social
        Problems* 29(5):524-531.

Macionis, John J.
1995   Sociology. New Jersey: Prentice Hall.

Mazess, Richard B.
1975   Biological Adaptation: Aptitudes and Acclimatization. *In*
        Biosocial Interrelations in Population Adaptation, eds. E.S.
        Watts et al. Pp. 9-18.

Melville, Keith
1983   Marriage and Family Today. 3d ed. New York: Random
        House.

Merton, Robert K.
1938   Social Structure and Anomie. *American Sociological Review.*
        3(6):672-82.

Metcoff, J.
1981   Fetal Growth Regulated by Maternal Nutrients. *Physiological
        and BiochemicalBasis for Perinatal Medicine.* 108-124.
        Samuel Z. Levine Conf., First International Meeting, Paris.
        Basel: Karger.

Metcoff, J., et al.
1985   Effect of Food Supplementation (WIC) During Pregnancy on
        Birth Weight. *American Journal of Clinical Nutrition*
        4:933-947.

Moon, Dreama G., Garry L. Rolison, Olayemi D. Akande, and Beverly
R. Fletcher
1994   Substance Abuse Among Female Prisoners in Oklahoma.
        *Journal of the Oklahoma Criminal Justice Resource
        Consortium* 1:23-32.

Moynihan, Daniel P.
1965   The Negro Family: The Case for National Action. U.S.
        Department of Labor, Office of Policy Planning and Research.
        Washington, DC.

Murray, Charles
1984   Losing Ground. New York: Basic.

National Center for Health Statistics
1968   Trends in Illegitimacy: United States, 1940-1965. *Vital and
        Health Statistics* 21(15). Washington, DC: Department of
        Health and Human Services

Nord, Christine Winquist, Kristin A. Moore, et al.
1992   Consequences of Teen-Age Parenting. *Journal of School
        Health.* 62(7): 310-317.

Office of the Governor
1974   Division of Economic Opportunity. *Poverty in Oklahoma.*
1981   Characteristics of the Poor: A Continuing Focus in Social
        Research. *Sociology and Social Research,* 65:323-331.

Oklahoma Department of Commerce
1995   *Statistical Abstract of Oklahoma.* Oklahoma City: Oklahoma
        Department of Commerce.

Oklahoma Employment Security Commission
1990   *Manpower Information for Affirmative Action Programs.*
        Oklahoma Employment Security Commission.
1991   Revised Data Through 1990 for: Payroll Employment and
        Wages. *Handbook of Employment Statistics* Vol. II. Oklahoma
        Security Commission.

Oklahoma State Department of Health
1992   Maternal Characteristics and Outcomes of Teenage Women in
        Oklahoma. *Oklahoma Prams-Gram: Pregnancy Risk
        Assessment Monitoring System.* 4(1):1.
1992   Unintended Pregnancy Among Live Births, Part I. *Oklahoma
        Prams-Gram: Pregnancy Risk Assessment Monitoring System.*
        3(3):1. Maternal & Child Health Service, Oklahoma State
        Department of Health

1994   Mother's Age at First Birth: Long Term Consequences of
        Early Childbearing. *Oklahoma Prams-Gram: Pregnancy Risk
        Assessment Monitoring System.* 4(1):1.

Oliker, Stacey J.
1994   The Proximate Contexts of Workfare and Work: A
        Framework for Studying Poor Women's Economic Choices.
        Paper presented at the 1994 American Sociological
        Association, Los Angeles, CA.

Olsen, Randall J. And George Farkas
1990   The Effect of Economic Opportunity and Family Background
        on Adolescent Cohabitation and Childbearing among
        Low-Income Blacks. *Journal of Labor Economics.*
        8(3):341-362.

Piven, Frances Fox and Richard A. Cloward
1971   Regulating the Poor. New York: Vintage.
1977   Poor People's Movements: Why They Succeed, Why They
        Fail. New York: Pantheon Books.

Rodgers, Joseph Lee and David C. Rowe
1993   Social Contagion and Adolescent Sexual Behavior: A
        Developmental EMOSA Model. *Psychological Review.*
        100(3):479-510.

Rothenberg, Paula S.
1992   Race, Class, and Gender in the United States: An Integrated
        Study. New York, NY: St. Martin's Press.

Sandhu, Harjit S., Hmoud Salem Al-Mosleh and Bill Chown
1994   Why Does Oklahoma Have the Highest Female Incarceration
        Rate in the U.S.? A Preliminary Investigation. *Journal of the
        Oklahoma Criminal Justice Resource Consortium* 1:13-22.

Segalen, Martine
1988   Historical nthropology of the Family. Cambridge: Cambridge
          University Press

Sewell, William
1971   Inequality of Opportunity for Higher Education. *American
          Sociological Review* 36:793-809.

Stack, Carol B.
1974   All Our Kin: Strategies for Survival in a Black Community.
          New York: Harper.

Sutherland, Edwin H., and Donald R. Cressey
1978   *Criminology.* 10th ed. Philadelphia: J.B. Lippincott.
          Tepperman, Lorne, and Susannah J. Wilson, eds.

Tepperman, Lorne and Susannah J. Wilson, eds.
1993   Next of Kin. Englewood Cliffs, NJ: Prentice Hall.

Thomas, Brooke R.
1994   Poverty and the Political Economy. Paper presented at the
          1994 American Anthropological Association Annual Meeting.
          Los Angeles, CA.

Thomas, Brooke R., Timothy B. Gage, and Michael A. Little
1979   Reflections on Adaptive and Ecological Models in *Human
          Population. Biology: A Transdiciplinary Science.* Haas and
          Little, eds. Oxford: Westview Press.

Thomas, R. Brooke, Bruce Winterhalder, and Stephen D. McRae.
1979   An Anthropological Approach to Human Ecology and
          Adaptive Dynamics. *Journal of Physical Anthropology
          Yearbook of Physical Anthropology.* 22:1-41.

Tilly, Louise A., and Joan W. Scott
1989   Women, Work & Family. New York: Routledge.

Tyree, Andrea, and Judith Treas
1974   The Occupational and Marital Mobility of Women. *American Sociological Review* 39:293-302.

United States Department of Commerce
1960a   Bureau of the Census, Census of Population, CP-Vol. 1, Part 38, *General Social and Economic Characteristics.* Washington, DC: Government Printing Office
1960b   Bureau of the Census, Census of Population, Supplementary Report, PC(S1)-54, *Poverty Areas in the 100 Largest Metropolitan Areas.* Washington, DC: Government Printing Office.
1990a   Bureau of the Census, Current Population Reports, Series P-60, No. 175, *Poverty in the United States: 1991.* Washington, DC: Government Printing Office.
1990b   Bureau of the Census, Census of Population, CP-Vol. 2, Part 38, *Social and Economic Characteristics.* Washington, DC: Government Printing Office.
1991   Bureau of the Census, Current Population Reports, Series P-60, No. 181, *Poverty in the United States: 1991.* Washington, DC: Government Printing Office.
1994   Bureau of Justice Statistics. *Sourcebook of Criminal Justice Statistics.* Washington, DC: Government Printing Services.

Upchurch, Dawn M. and James McCarthy
1990   The Timing of a First Birth and High School Completion. *American Sociological Review.* 55:224-234.

Veevers, Jean E.
1988   The Real Marriage Squeeze: Mate Selection, Mortality, and the Mating Gradient. *Sociological Perspectives* 31(1):169-189.

Weitzman, Lenore
1991   Divorce and the Illusion of Equality. *In* The Family
        Experience: A Reader in Cultural Diversity, ed. Hutter. Pp.
        243-280.

Williams, Terry M. and William Kornblum
1991   Sneakers Mothers. *In* The Family Experience: A Reader in
        Cultural Diversity, ed. Hutter. Pp. 589-600.

Wilson, William Julius
1987   The Truly Disadvantaged. Chicago: University of Chicago
        Press.
1991   Poverty and Family Structure: The Widening Gap Between
        Evidence and Public Policy Issues. *In* The Family Experience:
        A Reader in Cultural Diversity, ed Hutter. Pp. 204-231.

Index